Dear Kim

This is what I believe

Explaining Christian faith today
by Bill Loader

JBCE Specialty Books
Melbourne

Published by
THE JOINT BOARD OF CHRISTIAN EDUCATION
Second Floor, 10 Queen Street, Melbourne 3000, Australia

DEAR KIM: this is what I believe

National Library of Australia
Cataloguing-in-Publication entry.

Loader, William R. G. (William Ronald George), 1944-   .
Dear Kim: this is what I believe

ISBN: 0 85819 866 5.

1. Theology - 20th century. 2. Christian ethics. 3. Christianity - Essence, genius, nature. I. Joint Board of Christian Education. II. Title.

230

First printed 1993.

Design by Kelvin Young
Typeset by JBCE in Gatineau
Printed by Australian Print Group   JB93/3349

Contents

Preface

This book owes its name, Dear Kim, to a conversation I had with my niece during a recent trip to New Zealand. Kim asked me a number of questions about what I believe. Kim is a young adult in her early twenties. In the title of this book, however, Kim stands for a large number of adults known to me of all ages, and many more unknown to me, who stand either just inside or just outside the fringe of the Church and for whom many of the traditional answers of the Church no longer make sense.

I have endeavoured to address questions which I have heard and have sensed to be relevant for people today. I have not written this book for people who already have, or think they have, all the answers or who do not even want to ask the questions. I have in mind people like myself who are wanting to come to a deeper appreciation of what the Christian faith can mean when we are prepared to be open to the social, spiritual and intellectual movements of our time.

At the same time, I have deliberately restricted myself to writing a short book that cannot hope to tackle the issues in the depth they deserve. My comments are very much at the level of what I would say to Kim or others in conversation across the meal table. In this book you have to fill in the other side of the conversation - and many will be able to do so all too well! Perhaps some may go beyond that to find nourishment here and good wine. I hope so.

This is what I believe, without the kind of detailed explanation which would give the reader a sense of reading an elaborate defence. My aim has not been to be comprehensive nor to offer the kind of referencing and argument which belongs to a more academic treatment. I want, rather, to say something to my friends about what matters most to me. My friends are especially those, inside and outside the Church, who want to make sense of their faith in today's world.

Between the chapters I have also included a selection of stories and reflections which I have written over the years. They relate to the issues discussed but also express the faith that lies behind what I believe.

Finally I should like to thank Wendie Wilkie, Hazel Creagh, Revd Ian Tozer and members of my family who read the original draft and made helpful and encouraging comments. Thanks, too, to Chris for his help in the technical production. The final version has also been helped by the enthusiastic responses from listeners in a large number of parishes to whom I have presented these chapters as a series.

What about God?

Dear Kim

You asked me about God. I think about God in a number of different ways.

Sometimes I think of God as being like the life energy that is in everything. God is in everything. God is also in me and in you. I can be in tune with this life energy or out of tune with it. For me it has a lot to do with being at one with my true self. You know how sometimes you feel at odds with yourself or you know you're not really being true to yourself? Well, for me, that's the same as being true to God. I need to try to live in harmony with God and, if I do, then I'll live in harmony with my true self and with the world around me.

Conscience?

Some people call that conscience, but for me it's bigger than that. It's life; it's being in touch with the spirit and life of the universe. So it's much more than knowing what is right and wrong. It's a sense of oneness with myself, with nature, with other people. It is like knowing that they all draw on the same life energy - or they can. We all drink from the same stream. God is like the stream of life and love that flows through all things. I can let that flow in my life or I can block it. I can help it flow in the world or I can dam it up.

Sometimes I think of myself as a tree with my roots deep in the ground drawing up the moisture of that stream. The life moisture comes up into my being. When I think about it, I can sometimes even feel a physical sensation in my body as I relax at the thought. So it's important for me to make time every now and again to get in touch with my roots and to sense the sap flowing up into my body. It also helps me be aware of where I block that flow so I can decide to change things.

It's also a bit similar to that when I think of those around me and of the world of human beings. The life energy is about bringing harmony and wholeness. So, when I am in touch with it, I become more aware where there is disharmony, where the life stream is being blocked - in others, by others, by me, by us. So this is all connected with concern for peace among people, with concern for justice and equality, because the same spirit energy which wants to make me whole and healthy wants this also for the world of human beings.

I feel that also for the world of nature. I am connected with every other person and I am also connected with the world of nature. There's a sense in which what happens to them and to it happens to me. When I see nature savaged I feel a bit violated inside myself. When I see people treated like dirt, I feel dragged down too.

Behind everything

As well as thinking of God as being like the life energy in all things, I also think of God as behind everything. It's like saying: if it weren't for God, there wouldn't be anything; nothing would exist. You've probably felt a sense of wonder when you've looked at a tiny flower in all its beauty. Sometimes, out in the country at night, when the sky is really dark, I've looked out into the universe of stars and been struck by the vastness of it all: a huge endless array of worlds, stars, solar systems - and we see only a fraction of what there is! I find it hard to believe that there is not some intelligence behind it all. Something is behind all of this. I call that 'something' God.

The simplest way of expressing this is to say: 'God made the universe', but I'm not always sure that is so helpful. Immediately some people will think about the stories of creation in the Bible and take them literally. One of them says God created everything in six days. The other one says that humans were made like clay models and then breathed on and they came to life. These are ancient stories which have been preserved because of their deeper meaning, not because of their detail.

I'll say more about them when I talk about the Bible. I don't believe creation took place in six days. I'm not even sure that it makes a lot of sense to try to pin-point a beginning of time. But I do believe that God is the ultimate reason why there is not just nothing. So when I am close to the world around me, I feel close to God - and when I am close to God, I feel close to the world around me!

God as a person

When I talk about or think about God, I still prefer to speak of God as a person, not an 'it'. For me, being a person is more than being a thing. So, I can speak of God as the life energy of the universe, but I soon find myself speaking of God in much more personal terms. I've always been used to speaking of God as a person; it comes naturally; and I also want to keep doing it. But when I speak of God as a person, I am aware of how easily that can be misunderstood.

The main thing is: God must be greater than things and greater than persons. God must be quite different from things or people. Even to think of God as a being seems not quite right. It might be better to think of God as Being itself, Life itself. Yet that all sounds too abstract. We know what we are driving at, but any attempt to define God seems doomed to failure. That seems inevitable because of what or who God is! When the Old Testament says people should not make images of God, it seems to be aware of this point. When Moses asks what he should call God, he is told that God should be called: 'I am who I am'.

Shut up about God?

If we can't define or describe God, we should perhaps simply shut up - and that is not a bad idea at times, especially when people have been talking about God as if they know everything. If rabbits could think about God, they would probably think about God as a rabbit. Human persons think about God as a person. To do so is quite inadequate, but at least it is saying there is something in God I can relate to. It is better to say something than to say nothing about God. If I tried to remain silent, I would soon find myself inventing something.

I would find myself inventing something, because out of my inner self I find myself wanting to respond at a very deep level to God. There's a kind of primitive cry of thank you inside. Or sometimes there's a sense of awe and wonder at the magnificence of the universe. Or sometimes there's a sense of pain and anger which I feel God shares, too, at what goes on in the world. And some people with much harder life experiences than I have had would say: also a sense of pain and anger at what is happening to me. It is like there's a 'God frequency' inside along which the human heart expresses its deepest joy and pain.

Problems about God as a person

There are a number of problems in thinking of God in personal terms and some of them are big enough to turn people off religion altogether. Some people believe that God has plans for people's lives and sets those plans into action, like a puppeteer pulling strings. I don't think of God like that. Not that I think we are completely free to shape our own

9

destiny; we are much more shaped by what has gone on around us and by hereditary factors than we think. But that is very different from believing God has a detailed blueprint or that our fate is locked up in the stars.

For the same reason I also have difficulty with the idea that there is a God who pulls strings only sometimes, though I know that many people think this way. Some people understand prayer in this way: if I pray enough or rightly, God will alter the scheme of things for me (or for others): send the right weather, fix the car, find me a job, make me rich. It is easy (and probably a good thing) to poke fun at the self indulgence of many such prayers, but I don't want to overlook that many of these are prayers for others made out of love and concern.

The difficulty is that if we believe God intervenes in weather and the like in response to prayers, why doesn't God intervene in major famine and disaster areas? Is this 'God' unwilling, uncaring, needing more persuasion? This idea of God makes little sense to me and I am not comforted by the explanation that it is all part of a plan which I shall finally understand in the next world. I find it hard therefore to make sense of people saying God saved them from a motor accident or 'took someone' through a motor accident or cancer or the like. It might help people to accept and come to terms with what has happened by saying it was 'meant to be', but it does not fit my understanding of God. I am not being irreverent about God; I am being irreverent, perhaps, about people's ideas of God.

Love, making room and staying in touch

I prefer to think of God as having set the universe free to evolve and develop in its own way and that the magic of the universe is that forms of intelligence have evolved which can have an active part in shaping that development. To picture it in a mythical way, God has chosen not to take up the whole space, but has made room for others and made room for them to develop and evolve in their own way. God gives the world this freedom. Love means making room for others to be, giving them space and staying in touch. God stays in touch with the universe.

But how does God stay in touch with the universe? At one level I want to answer: I do not know and cannot know. Maybe we are encountering God not only in enjoying the universe, but also when we suffer the backlash of treating it badly, like it is a giant organism capable of repelling danger. Is that God or is that simply reaping the fruit of our own actions?

10

On the other hand, I find it absurd to think of God as just a kind of spectator, sitting in the stand, as it were, biting his or her nails in anxiety and compassion, hoping good wins in the field of human endeavour. God might as well not exist, if God is only to be thought of as the one who started the ball rolling and then left it to its fate.

So it makes sense to me to think of God as deeply involved with the universe, but not as someone looking on from outside and occasionally switching the controls when the right message comes in. Rather God is inside, within us, among us, seeking to bring life, love and peace to us and our world. We can know ourselves to be sharing in that life and love. We are partners with God in the ongoing development of the universe - in our own minute but significant way. Praying means deliberately seeking out this connection with God, taking time and making space in our lives to open our lives to God, soaking up the love energy from the roots up. God is in there with us - in joy, in struggle, in pain, in adventure, in creativity.

It also makes sense to me to think of praying for others as being a channel of God's love and energy for others. I think of this less as my trying to persuade God to do something and more as my opening myself to God's persuasion, to be part of God's loving to others. I'm not really sure how this works, but there seems sometimes to be a connection between a praying person and the person or persons prayed for which is beneficial and I find this a way of understanding what happens when we pray.

Underlying everything I have said so far is an important assumption: that God (whatever it or he or she is) is good and not bad. It is possible to imagine a bad god, like one of those evil monster figures out of space science fiction: some hoary evil genius on a distant planet having fun with humans, kidding them there is hope when there is no hope. Life is just one big, bad joke. Many people's experience of life is not far from that.

But nor is God an old doting grandpa or grandma sitting on a golden throne up in the sky. That's all part of the problem in thinking of God as a person. When we think of God as a person, we inevitably think of God in human imagery. Thinking of God as a wise old man or woman isn't too bad an image! But mostly what has happened is that people have thought of the highest and best human being they can think of and then used that as the image for God. This can be enlightening or quite misleading. Let me illustrate what I mean.

11

Human images of God: good news and bad news

In most societies the most honoured person was usually the ruler, the most powerful, and, inevitably, male. Therefore people thought of God as king. A king sits on a throne; people bow before a king; a king should be obeyed without question, if he is a good king. And in families the most honoured person, the head of the house was the father. Therefore people thought of God as a father. It is all very male oriented and very power oriented.

As people thought of God in these ways, two things happened simultaneously. The human models of what was important affected people's understanding of God and, in turn, people's understanding of God reinforced the human models of power in society and in the family. People were quite happy to picture God as king and father of the universe. If their understanding of kings and fathers was cruel and destructive, they happily attributed these qualities to God.

However one of the dominant models for thinking about God as a king and father, which reflected people's ideals of human kings and fathers, was that of the benevolent dictator. This king retained his power and honour, but provided ways for his subjects to regain favour when they had wronged him. If they came to him in repentance and perhaps offered some other guarantees, they could be forgiven.

If we use the model of God as a benevolent dictator, we can produce an account of the gospel which sounds something like this. God the king had disobedient subjects who had offended him by transgressing his laws, but he looked for a way of making an exception by giving them a second chance. Jesus is pictured as the king's own son. He offers the king a way out which doesn't compromise the king's dignity and his laws. In an act of voluntary obedience, he allowed himself to become a substitute for others and to take the punishment due to them. This transaction freed the king to forgive people without compromising his strict laws of reward and punishment. This system and its benefits applied however only for an interim period. In the long term the king would subject those who crossed him or rejected his system to everlasting torment. The father would shut the door on these children forever. But this king's violence was justified, because he was 'God' and because his laws by which all were judged were just. Seen from the perspective of the whole, the act of compassion in making forgiveness possible was only a temporary interim measure and an exception to the king's normal behaviour.

12

Images of power and violence or images of compassion

Many people have drawn up the message of Christianity on the basis of this model. It is meant to be 'good news', but, on the other side of the coin, it is really bad news: it teaches that human beings are ultimately dispensible; in the long run they can be written off; it teaches that violence is justified against people if my cause is right, because 'God' is like that in the end; and it teaches that ultimately forgiveness is only a concession without surrender of power. Many major ills of our society reflect this side of the coin. It is not surprising that where this norm has held its sway, many forms of violence have flourished: international, institutional, domestic, interpersonal.

Unfortunately, within the stream of Christian tradition over the ages, this current of thought has nearly always been present. Yet, to me, it is a gross misrepresentation and distortion of what I understand the gospel to be. Even on the side of the coin where it is supposed to be good news, it remains bad news. In fact, I would claim, that the good news is that I can abandon that way of thinking about God. There are two reasons why I say this, one modern and one ancient.

First, our understanding of kings and fathers has changed. Our understanding of what are the best human models has changed. To begin with, why use a male image? Why not a female? God is not a 'he' or a 'she'. But, more than that, we are learning to see power in a new way. No one has the right to do violence to another person. That is not because everyone has their faults and only a perfect person would have such a right (like a god). It is the violence itself which we have learned is wrong. The most enlightened legal systems penalise only with a view to learning, restitution and rehabilitation.

These days we see government less in terms of rulers who have a right to power because of their strength or their virtue or their breeding and more as people elected to act for the interests of all. Compassion and caring is their agenda and we rightly complain when it is not there and when people seem to be in politics just for the sake of power. We look on compassion and caring as the norm to be expected, not as some hoped-for concession to be bartered from the ruler by transaction or special pleading. It is the people whose lives are marked by generosity and compassion whom we have learned to honour, not those with claims to self importance on the basis of aristocracy, wealth and power.

This also affects the way I understand prayer. In ancient society rulers were largely preoccupied with their own interests. If you wanted something done for yourself or for someone else you needed to petition the monarch; otherwise the monarch is not likely to take any interest or undertake any initiative. This has influenced people's understanding of prayer: 'God' needs to be distracted from 'his' own interests and concerns to give attention to human beings. When, however, I start thinking about God as being always attentive and loving, I start seeing prayer in a different way. It has less to do with getting God to tune in to me and more to do with my tuning in to God and being available to be a channel of God's continuing love and compassion in the world.

Forgiveness a concession or a form of loving?

Similarly, our understanding of human relationships has changed significantly. Forgiveness is not a concession on the basis of sufficient remorse being shown, but something we give freely. Forgiveness is giving up of power; it is when we no longer hold something, ourselves, back from someone or hold something against them. Fathers - and mothers - who maintain relationships with their children primarily on the basis of claiming their rights to respect and obedience are impoverishing themselves and their children. I would hate to be respected by my children on that kind of basis - it is so distant.

It is not power and fear, but love that makes relationships work best. The kind of respect I want is the same I want to give to everyone else and want for them: to see other people as unique individuals, to respect their right to their own decisions, to honour their boundaries, to meet them with who I am and what I need and have to give.

I would be shocked into serious self-examination if someone thought I needed to be appeased or persuaded before I would respond to others in love, as though I were somehow above loving or had a right to withhold love. I would be even more appalled if in response to my loving, people argued I should be praised because I went beyond what is to be expected. Yet it is precisely this which I find regularly in expressions of Christian piety. People don't want to believe that God actually wants to be loving and wants us to expect that love. At worst it is like they are saying: thank you for loving and forgiving us, because when you are your usual self we can only expect you to be quite uncaring and cold.

When we praise God's love as unexpected and exceptional, we subtly reinforce our dominant value system, that ultimately what matters most is power and dignity not love and we show that we do not really believe in love. Our problem, in part, is that much of our language in church is drawn from the imagery of courts and kings and we find it hard not to be drawn into the value systems which that traditionally represents.

What I am saying is that on the two models which have been most influential for thinking about God, rulers and fathers, we have moved such a long way from the understanding which underlies the picture I outlined above. I am quite concerned, however, that many people still operate with a model of God which depends on human models no longer defensible in our world.

Jesus shows us a better way

There is a more ancient reason why we need an alternative model of God to the one parodied above. For my plea is only partly that we update our thinking about God. I also want us to 'backdate' it. I mean we need to backdate it to Jesus, because, despite the strength of the other model in his context, Jesus shows us a better way of understanding God. From Jesus I learn that compassion and caring are not exceptions to the norm in the life of God, but they are the way God is, was and always will be. God doesn't need a transaction to be able to forgive and stay consistent with the law; God's being and nature is to want to bring life and wholeness; and forgiveness and restoration are part of that.

Am I suggesting we abandon worshipping and honouring God? Are we to abandon reverence, the 'fear of the Lord'? But then what is worship and honour? For me, honouring any person means acknowledging them for who they are, respecting that they are different from me, that I can never presume to know everything about them. It means having a sense of awe before others as I realise their mystery, their distinctiveness, and treating them as holy. This is the most I can give to others and the most I want for myself. It is also the most I can be for God and, I believe, the most God wants. Worship is opening myself to what I know God to be and letting myself sense something of what that means. My response may be one of silence, of awe, of praise, of singing, of joy or pain. I am in the presence of the love which gave birth to the universe. That is far from the image of a power-obsessed deity demanding fear.

God is not a super-king or super-father bent on cowering 'his' subjects or children to respect and obedience; God is like Jesus. Jesus, by what he said and what he did, turned the popular power-based image of God upside down. It is significant that the kind of parent model Jesus speaks of is of one who runs down the road to embrace a wayward son with compassion. And the kind of king imagery in the gospel story is of

Jesus crowned with thorns on a cross. Here is a new kind of power, an apparently foolish and powerless power. Here is the love that brought it all into being and which never gives up in its yearning to bring justice and wholeness to the world.

So when you ask me about God, I can't help but go on to talk about Jesus.

ooo

God and the sparrows

Long ago before there was anything at all, God existed alone with two angels. One day the three of them were sitting together in contemplative mood.

The first angel spoke: 'Why don't you make something, God? Why don't you create, set up some new reality beside yourself? Let there be a universe of expanding stars and galaxies, planets and an earth, where life's energy can evolve miracles of shape and size and colour: plants and trees, birds and reptiles, beings of all sorts, beings who might one day look to you as their companion, who might enjoy all you are and all you have done.'

God sat back and contemplated.

Then the other angel spoke: 'No,' it said, 'don't embark on such a plan. You have no idea what could come of it. Just imagine such things moving about, crashing into one another, combining into all kinds of evil: disease, tiny organisms to destroy, landscapes to buckle and crack, weather patterns to play havoc, beings to fight each other, and who knows there may evolve out of all this mess your own worst enemies who will despise you and all you have done!'

God sat back and contemplated, weighing the dangers and the opportunities.

Love welled up in God's being and suddenly it happened. There was an enormous explosion. Out of nothing in a split second had come a scattering newness, fragments of beginning racing into the unknown, creating their own space, burning with possibility.

Galaxies evolved, stars, solar systems and there among the planets began the miracles of life. Slimey primordial life made its upward way. From chaos emerged the shapes and forms that struggled for survival, the grasses, the plants, the trees, the reptiles, the birds, the kangaroos and all living mammals; and evolving over hundreds of millions of years the upright figure of humankind, people who dreamed dreams and thought thoughts and imagined God.

So it began and so it continued for many, many years.

Then one day outside a bustling city just before dusk on a deserted skull shaped hill there was a return to primordial silence. The crowds who had thronged that place had gone. On the hill was a cross and there were two sparrows. One was busy with the pickings of the day, flies drawn to spilt blood and to torn shreds of clothing. Soon it was off with the beginnings of a new nest. The other remained motionless for a long time. Then finally it flew up and perched on the cross bar. Turning to heaven it said: 'I told you. I told you.'

From heaven came a deeply sad and yet determined reply: 'I know. I know.'

ooo

17

What about Jesus?

Dear Kim

There are so many questions you ask about Jesus. Let me begin by saying that Jesus was a Jewish man who lived at a particular time of human history which we know something about. It was the time of the Roman Empire and the place where he lived was Palestine. In other words, whatever else I or any other person may say, Jesus was a figure in human history, not a god nor a legendary or mythical figure. Nor is he someone made up by religious people; otherwise it would be too difficult to explain the various contradictions which exist in the accounts of his life. And, apart from that, non-Christian sources of the first two centuries (for example, Josephus, Tacitus) treat him like any other historical figure.

So much has been said about Jesus down through the centuries that it is often hard to get a picture of what he was really like. There is much legend and symbol that has grown up around him, but behind it all there is a real human person, Jesus.

Light shining through

Sometimes I think of human history as being like a very large rug with a light under it in a dark room. I'm thinking of the kind of rug where here and there the light could actually shine through - a holey rug! The light shines through at a number of places. I think God is like that light in human history.

The light breaks through at a number of points in human history where something happens or someone says some thing and people say: hey, that really opened up something for me; that was a revelation; I see life in a new way now; that was a God-moment; like, I caught a glimpse of what really matters in life. Or maybe they just sense something without being able to put it into words.

This has happened at many points in history and in many cultures. And it can happen for each of us. Occasionally it is so significant that we remember it as a turning point in our lives, when everything came together, when the penny dropped, when we saw the light. It may be prompted by a tragedy, a high point, or just some very ordinary occurrence or through something someone else said or did.

When an event like this happens for communities of people, they often celebrate it for years to come. It needn't always be a pleasant experience. Australians and New Zealanders treat the disaster at Gallipoli during the First World War as an event like this. Legends build up around such experiences. There are rituals and ceremonies, too. And the funny thing is that it is often hard to put your finger on why the occasion was so important. Why make such a big thing of one of the ANZAC's biggest failures? Is it because people realised how much they needed each other? Is it because we all feel one with those who are hard up against it? Was that the revelation?

Religions often grow up around such events or stories, especially when the events happened long ago. In religions, people usually try to get back in touch with important events like this. They sing about them, talk about them, sometimes even dance them or try to reenact them. In most religions you can usually find they celebrate a series of major events like this. The Jews celebrate the liberation of their people from Egypt in the annual Passover meal. The Old Testament of the Bible includes accounts of such events which were significant for the people, Israel.

Jesus and the light shining through

When I look over the rug for signs of God shining through in human history, for me the brightest spot is the life of Jesus. All of the others are important, but, for me, it's at this point where I see something unique and special. I use Jesus as my major clue for understanding God and the universe. When I say 'Jesus', I am really referring only to a short period of his life just before his death, three years or perhaps even less than a year, the period covered by the gospels. And I am referring to the impression he left on those around him, especially as it is preserved in what they remembered about him. The data base is fairly small, but big enough to get an overall picture.

What do I see in Jesus? Before I answer that, let me recap: what am I looking for? I am looking for what God is like, what life is all about. I am wanting to get in touch with what lies behind the universe, what makes sense of it, what ultimately matters. These are all God-type questions. What do I see when I look at the data we have on Jesus?

19

The first thing that I see is that Jesus taught that God is loving and compassionate towards all people. Nothing stands in the way of that love and respect for people, not their race, their religion, their sex, their age, not even if they are people who are the worst rogues under the sun. Nothing indicates that Jesus was blind to all these differences or naively pretended everyone was good and therefore deserved loving. On the contrary his love was honest and straight. He came face to face with an immoral swindler, but was not prepared to write him off. He wrote no-one off. Contrary to the attitudes of many in his day, he treated women as equals, he welcomed outcasts, he valued people considered small and insignificant, including children.

Jesus lived what he taught

In other words, Jesus lived out in his life what he taught and what he believed about God. Without making a big thing of it, he claimed to be reflecting God's own attitudes in what he said and did. You can see that in the stories he told. One tells of a father. This father had a son who wheedled out of him the share of his father's fortune he would have inherited when his father died. He went off with all this money, made a right mess of his life and then had the audacity to turn up again at his father's homestead. What did the father do? Shut the door on his son or, at least, make sure first that he had mended his ways? No. The father did what any decent father would do: when he saw his son coming, he was filled with compassion, got up, ran down the road and embraced him. That's how we ought to think of God, said Jesus. Jesus' portrait of this father is provocative, because it broke the cultural norms according to which fathers should be seen to act with dignity and reserve. For Jesus, God does not play the power games of dignity and reserve.

Jesus used stories of human love and compassion like this as his model for God. God is not like an offended father or mother who says: 'I never want to see you again'; or: 'I'll only accept you back if you make amends!' Nor is Jesus' picture of God one of a king or ruler obsessed with getting everyone to bow and scrape before him. Jesus does use the traditional language of king to refer to God; he even lives by a vision of a day when God will reign over all in the universe. But the picture of this reign is a picture not of subjugation to a tyrant, but of human beings living in a loving community, eating and drinking together in peace, enjoying each other and enjoying oneness with God.

The vision and the reality

Jesus appears to have used a common vision of how things could be when God reigns, as a blueprint for his own lifestyle. This makes sense because if you live by a picture of how it will be when God reigns, then that is the same as letting God reign in your life now. And letting God reign or rule in your life now is just another way of saying: living in a way that is in touch with God. Or we could say: letting God's energy and spirit have its way in your life. In that sense we are also talking about what it means to live fully as a human being. Being truly human means letting the love and compassion of God that is within and behind the universe flow through your life.

You can see the way this works out when Jesus talks about various aspects of human life. People were concerned about what was right and wrong. He changed the direction of their thinking. They looked at the commandments. Jesus looked beyond them. So instead of just saying, 'Don't murder', Jesus said: 'Don't write people off at all, not even by your thoughts.' Similarly instead of talking about adultery, he taught that any sexual exploitation of women is wrong, whether it is in your action or just in your attitude. He attacked the divorce system of the day which drove many women into poverty. He called for straight honesty in relationships and went so far as arguing that no situation justifies your writing anyone off, not even if the person is your worst enemy. The attitude of treating others as people of worth runs through everything he said and did.

Putting this kind of radical love at the heart of his thinking about God and at the heart of his practical living brought Jesus into conflict with many of his contemporaries. He was a practising Jew, but sat lightly to many of its ritual and cultic rules, especially where human need was concerned. He wasn't anti religious, but he saw rites and rituals as an aid to what was the central thing: helping people become one with God and live at one with others.

Jesus' lifestyle and God's lifestyle

Jesus probably had his own characteristic rituals and practices. One of them seems to have been giving meals a special significance as times of sharing and belonging together. The church's practice of Holy Communion stems ultimately from Jesus' own practice. He seems to have openly shared meals with all sorts of people, from the pious and respectable to the rogue and outcast. These were occasions of acceptance and celebration flowing from his strong belief in God's love for all. Another of his characteristics was his simple lifestyle: he had a small band of women and men who travelled around with him and they all shared a common purse for daily needs.

He appears also to have had the ability to heal people. Miracle stories are often legendary and it is always hard to tell fact from pious fiction. Some stories, like those about Jesus walking on water and stilling storms, probably reflect pictures people drew of Jesus after the event rather than actual occurrences. They are powerfully symbolic. But there is probably a kernel of stories that go back to Jesus' activity as a successful faith healer.

The primary thing about Jesus was his claim to be living out the way God wants us to be. It was precisely because Jesus was truly human in this sense that we say he was truly God. He never said anything like: I am God. But it is not wide of the mark when people said to meet him was like meeting God. After all, he was a window on what God is like. That is what they believed and what I believe. The earliest Christian writer, Paul, said: 'God was in Christ'; and later Church shorthand simply said: he was God. But they never meant for one moment that he was not an ordinary human being like you and me.

Jesus' public execution

Jesus stuck with his conviction about God. His life ended in a gruesome public execution. The Romans killed him by their usual method: crucifixion. They nailed him up on a wooden cross along with others they considered criminals, with the charges against them hung over their heads for all to see. It was a common method of deterring crime. For them he was probably just another statistic. Crucifixions were common.

The Romans had probably been fed information by the temple authorities in Jerusalem that Jesus should be considered dangerous. The present accounts of Jesus' trial and death in the gospels are so much shaped by the Christians' own later encounter with Jewish and Roman courts that it is almost impossible to reconstruct what really happened in Jesus' last days. Maybe the Romans considered any movement that was growing in momentum as suspicious. The Jews had been producing a number of popular movements, many of which were directly anti-Roman. Perhaps Jesus' rather confrontational approach to the hierarchical temple system in Jerusalem, where the rich and powerful held sway, tipped the scales against him. The Romans perhaps saw any destabilising of the temple as an action against their own interests.

It was a mixture of political and religious concerns that removed Jesus. Jesus and his message of love had the capacity to transform people's attitudes, to offer individuals new hope and to set the agenda for a just and peaceful world. But he was snuffed out - almost by accident, a victim of the political and religious fears of his day. It is hardly fair to say the Jews as a people killed him; it was the political and religious authorities

The cross, a symbol of love

But when we look back, we see that the killing of Jesus becomes one of those big events where lots of things come together. Here was love which kept loving right to the end. One account of his death even has him pray for his killers while he hung on the cross; he kept true to loving to the end. This was a revelation of love. The cross became a symbol of this love. It became a symbol of God.

In a fascinating way it turned traditional values upside down. The Romans soldiers ridiculed Jesus by dressing him up as a king. The charge against him was that he was wanting to be a king of the Jews. That charge hung above him on the cross. It was false. Yet people soon realised that at another level it was true; Jesus had shown what being a king really means. He showed what kind of king God is: not a king of power, but a king of love. This challenges all prevailing systems of power which think 'might is right'. The powerful powerlessness of the cross has been an amazing symbol.

The cross, a symbol of evil

The other side of the coin is that the event of Jesus' death has become a symbol of what is evil: the killing of love, wherever it occurs and whatever justification people use to excuse it. The justification in Jesus' case was the need to keep law and order, to maintain stability on the eastern flank of the Roman empire. Sadly, people always seem to find a way of justifying the destruction of love and justice. The cry for law and order is frequently the impulse for actions which lead to the violation of human rights.

Jesus' suffering was not greater than that of other human beings. Many have suffered far worse. But it is the fact that human beings conspired together to kill someone so unique as Jesus that is the horror of the event. People snuffed out the brightest and clearest expression of love the world has ever seen. It was a crime not only against him, but against all humanity, and ultimately against God. So, as well as being a revelation of the best in humankind, love, it is also a revelation of the worst in humankind, a symbol of evil.

The death of Jesus, therefore, is one of those events which makes waves. It continues to make an impact across history right into the present day. In one way it sums up what Jesus' life was all about because it shows he loved to the end. It is a symbol of his life. Paul, later, could sum up all that Christianity was about by speaking simply of 'the cross'; he preached 'the cross'.

It has become a symbol of the central issues in all human life: do I kill the love which wants to be alive in me? Each of us knows how to crucify love in ourselves and in our world. So the words of the spiritual ask: 'Were you there when they crucified my Lord?'

Finding our way into the story

If we keep coming back to this event, we can keep in touch better with what is happening in our own lives and in our world. When they function well, Christian communities help us feel our way back into the story - whether we are on the side of the crucifiers or the crucified. That alerts us to what is going on around us and within us and we can get in touch again with what that love is all about.

A uniquely powerful event like this explodes into the world with so much energy that no human imagery of explanation can really sum it up. Little wonder that one of the earliest Christian responses was to say: Christ died for us, for our sins. The wrong we do, our lovelessness, has been foisted onto this human being. They experienced this event as a source of enormous healing for their own lives. The goodness concentrated in this event overflows to the benefit of all. It was like he died as a representative of all human beings.

In a world where temples and sacrifices were common it is not surprising that people began to speak of Jesus' death as being like a sacrifice which removed guilt and impurity. They spoke of the healing power of his sacrifical blood. It is strange to our ears. They understood themselves to have been cleansed by the blood of Jesus. This was their way of talking about the impact of Jesus' death, or better of his life and death. It has been off-putting for many that some Christians have persisted in using such language in modern society where temples and sacrifices are no longer part of our common way of life. There are lots of other ways of talking about the impact of Jesus than to speak in the language of blood and sacrifices, but we can know what they meant and share their faith.

Resurrection

It is possible to think of Jesus and his impact as simply an event in history of enormous, even unique, significance. The first Christians went further than that. Their understanding of life included life after death, and especially resurrection. By resurrection they meant that a person begins a new form of existence at a different level of reality. Usually they envisaged this transformed life as entailing a transformation of the dead corpse into a new spiritual reality. This belief went along with the hope that ultimately everything would be transformed to the new level of existence. Some saw it all happening at a set time in the future. Others saw it as something which could start happening already in the present. The details of such beliefs are somewhat vague, but they form the backdrop for the earliest Christians' first great claim about Jesus.

Our earliest Christian sources speak of Peter, one of Jesus' disciples, coming to a new startling belief: instead of remaining in the sleep of death like other human beings who had died, Jesus had been resurrected and Peter had glimpsed him in this new state. Unfortunately there is no description anywhere in earliest writings of what exactly Peter saw, but apparently others had similar visual experiences, women and men. Some accounts even have women as the first to have had the experience. The conviction that God had raised Jesus to the new level of existence became fundamental for Christian faith and turned dejected men and women, disappointed at his death, into enthusiastic propagators of Jesus and his message.

Inevitably this belief called out for further elaboration. The pictures drawn for us in the New Testament vary considerably. Sometimes we read of Jesus walking about and talking as though an actual resuscitation had taken place and he had a normal body of flesh and blood. Others are more careful and speak of appearances and revelations. In all four gospels there is an account of Jesus' tomb being empty. The assumption here is that the corpse of Jesus had been transformed into the new reality. It is difficult to be sure whether this story grew out of the conviction that Jesus was alive or whether it represents memory of finding the tomb actually empty. I'm inclined to the former view; but on the central issue I want to affirm: I believe that Jesus is more than a figure of past history. I believe he belonged to God in his life and I find it hard to believe that he does not belong to God now.

Using very personal language of God, we could say that God raised Jesus from the dead and took him home. He is with God. One of the earliest claims was that God had given Jesus a seat on God's right hand side in heaven. He was to reign as king. If we try to translate these images into other language we could say: Jesus is alive with God and God has elevated him to the most important position in the universe. God has said 'yes' to all that Jesus said and did. This is a way of saying that Jesus truly is what he claimed to be. What he said about God and what he lived out in his life is true. He is the place where the light shines through.

Jesus as good news

You can imagine that now the earliest Christian community had a message that had something extra. They still preached and taught what Jesus had said and done; but, added to that, they had the message of his death and his resurrection. In the years that followed they went out and about through their native Judea and Galilee, then spread north to Syria, across to Greece, over to Rome, south to Egypt, and finally throughout the Mediterranean world and also towards the east. They met many different cultures. They were safe most of the time speaking the common Greek language, but, even then, cultures differed considerably. How could they speak about Jesus to people with very different backgrounds from their own without losing the central thrust of what were Jesus' concerns?

This continues to be a major task for people who are part of the continuing Jesus movement; otherwise the message of Jesus gets lost in a ghetto community with its own in-group language and strange ceremonies and institutions and loses relevance for the world around it. One of the reasons I'm writing this book is that I fear this has been happening too much in recent years.

How could people convey the magic of what Jesus was on about? The disciples tried almost everything. Many Christians became obsessed with Jesus as an authority and lost sight of his message. At worst they were in danger of heaping onto Jesus all the honourable titles they could lay hands on. But such devotion easily produced a Jesus looking quite the opposite of the Jesus of the earliest records: a stern royal ruler rather than a humble caring human being. This is just another version of people

26

foisting onto God (Jesus, in this case) their own value systems. It is too easily forgotten that the earliest setting of royal imagery for Jesus is the imagery of irony: the crowned crucified Jesus.

Terms like Son of God and Lord became popular. They can carry positive and negative connotations depending of how much of the story of the real Jesus is remembered. Son of God came to be a way of saying that Jesus belongs to God's family. That is an image which tries to grasp the intimate link between Jesus and God. If any human being is son of God, Jesus is and more. This fits well with his tender language about God being like a caring father and with his special closeness to God. On the other hand, it is quite misleading to take the language literally as if we must insert God into Jesus' family tree. The wonderful legends of Jesus' birth to a virgin should not be used in this way. They represent in a fabled way an attempt to say that God meant Jesus to be the way he was and had a hand in it from the beginning.

Other Christians soon used popular mythology as a way of expressing the truth about Jesus. Some circles used to speak of Wisdom (Greek: Sophia) as God's partner and assistant in the creation and ordering of the universe. It is not always clear whether they were thinking of an actual being, like an angel, or just using personal imagery. Wisdom is often pictured as a woman. Some linked the figure with God's Law or God's Word, the Jewish scriptures. Others defined it in such a way that it represented what humans could grasp of God: the image or likeness of God. It was also seen as something like the meaning that holds all of reality together.

For Christians Jesus was now the meaning that held the universe together. He was the image and likeness of God. He was God's Word. As such they also found it easy to say that the one we see in Jesus was in the universe from the beginning. In the historical Jesus we see this one taking on human flesh and blood.

When words and explanations fail

In all these attempts categories failed to grasp adequately what had happened and what people believed. The event was larger and more significant than could simply be put into words. In the long run the Church fixed certain pegs of belief in the ground and left the rest to flap, so to speak, but the tent of faith it erected was enough to shelter what people cherished. Those pegs included: Jesus was a real human being, not just one on the outside. He really did live and die at a particular time and place in human history. It really was God whom people encountered in Jesus, not a second god, not an angel or some other kind of being.

For me, to say Jesus is human means I believe that he was not a walking encyclopedia, knowing everything from his birth onwards. He was a human being of his time, living under usual human limitations of knowledge and education. He doubtless believed in a world populated by demons like his contemporaries and probably believed the world was more or less flat, with the sky as a dome in which the stars and moon shone by night and the sun by day, the common Old Testament picture. His expectations about history were those of his time. He lived in a community which thought history was soon coming to an end. His healing practices reflect the methods of his world.

In his particular time and place and culture, however, I believe he was in touch with God like no one else I know. He expressed this reality in the world of his time and as a person of his time. He was genuinely human. I believe this also with regard to what he was able and not able to do. I cannot think of him as a human being carrying around with him, as it were, a divine power pack of cosmic proportions. He was not a superman.

Sinless?

Another motif commonly linked with the picture of Jesus is that of his sinlessness. People who preferred the language of sacrifice to speak of Jesus' death highlighted this. A sacrifice had to be spotless and perfect. He was spotless and perfect. Others hailed Jesus as the righteous one as a way of declaring their belief that Jesus was truly speaking and acting in harmony with God. Unfortunately, later centuries extrapolated from this that Jesus was sinless in a statistical sense and even had to be - from the cradle. This gave rise to legends of his childhood where he acts in total maturity. Later, artists were even inclined to portray the baby Jesus with a grown up's face.

To my mind nothing in the early tradition demands that we should believe Jesus was anything other than a normal child and adolescent. I find it quite compatible with my faith to believe that Jesus, too, will have had to learn by his mistakes and will have had the usual ups and downs characteristic of being human in this world. Certainly, the gospels do not shy away from picturing him as having experiences of human sadness and anxiety. The portrait of Jesus bent in agony in Gethsemane and of crying out words of despair on the cross should hold the peg firm against any attempts to make a superman out of him. Jesus struggled. And there, too, he opens a window for us. Yet, I still hear Christians saying (and singing) that if you're on God's side your life will be trouble free!

The Trinity

One of the structures linking some of these pegs, which the Church hammered in to hold together its belief, is the doctrine of the Trinity. It says God is three: the Father, the Son and the Holy Spirit; and these three are one. On the surface it is a contradiction: how can three be one! Yet it is an attempt to hold together some essential ideas which don't fit together well and yet which seem to belong. On the one side, all our talk about God in Jesus must never lead to the idea that there is more than one God. On the other side, Jesus cannot be described just simply as God; otherwise he is hardly a human being. The third figure, the Spirit, is also sometimes spoken of separately: for example, God sent the Spirit. The one we meet in all is the one God, yet the language allows for three figures to be spoken of.

In many ways the problem seems easier to solve with the Spirit which is perhaps best taken as just another way of speaking of God in a particular mode of relating. The word, Spirit (old English used 'Ghost'), goes back to Greek and Hebrew words which mean spirit, breath and wind. Spirit can be a more intimate way of speaking of God, like God's breath. Traditionally it is also a way of describing God's creative power bringing about new possibilities and realising future hopes and visions.

With Jesus things are considerably more complicated. Is he a combination of a human being and something else, namely, God? Did he have two personalities? I find most of this rather meaningless speculation. Perhaps we shall never be able to offer an adequate explanation. I prefer to understand Jesus' relationship to God, exemplified by his praying to God, primarily as one of total human devotion and to avoid theories which demand some kind of shared combination of beings in the human Jesus. It was precisely because he was such an in-touch human being that God shone through his life uniquely.

Yet in general people make no difference between Jesus and God when they think about the present living Jesus. One person prays to Jesus, another to God, the Father. Really both are praying to God. This has made it easier for people to say simply, Jesus is God. To be in touch with Jesus is to be in touch with God. So thinking of Jesus in history leads us to stress his humanity, while thinking of Jesus in the present leads to a stronger emphasis on his divinity. The creeds of the church seek to hold onto both aspects.

Some people get excited by abstract models of God as a single community of beings, but I must say I find this too abstruse. I'm happier with what some of the traditional structures are meant to affirm than I am with what people think they affirm when they work with them in a more literal way. A lot of the problems which have arisen in such speculative discussions have come about because of the popularity of one particular model of thought about Jesus in the time leading up to when the creeds were written, especially from the second century of Christianity onwards.

Just a set of good ideas?

I am also unhappy with attempts to reduce Christianity to just a set of good ideas like 'love' or 'justice and peace'. I'm not against trying to abstract and summarise - I'm doing it here - but I'm convinced that events of deep meaning, like the event of Jesus, need to be left intact. They need to be left in their historical and cultural setting, because it is only there that we can encounter them in anything like their full depth. When you try to crystallise out from them a few central ideas, you lose something. This is so for many of our own personal life experiences. There are things we cannot put into words; the nearest thing we can do is say what happened, tell a story, try to re-present the event in some way.

Events are more than ideas. They have flesh and blood. We can read of events or see them on film or in theatre and feel caught up into them in a way that never happens with ideas on their own. They have a way of entering our experience; we can find ourselves entering them and becoming part of theirs. This is what I meant before in quoting the words of the spiritual: 'Were you there when they crucified my Lord?' When people think about that event, they often find that they are represented there in what happened.

For many, the story of how Jesus openly faced suffering, pain and death and then found life in the resurrection, has become a model for their own lives. Many would say it was only when they faced up to their own pain (or fear or guilt or hurt) that they came through to a new start in life. Jesus' death and resurrection becomes a model of what works for their own lives. In the same way others have found that it was as they gave up hanging onto their lives selfishly and let themselves love that

30

they moved from being dead to being alive. Jesus' death becomes a model and also a stimulus which changes people's life-patterns. The impact of Jesus' life left an impression on those around him. That impression has been preserved for us in the Church's traditions. This is the only picture of Jesus we have, but it is one still capable of transforming people's lives and attitudes. The lofty doctrines and elaborate imagery which arose over the course of time around this picture are important, but they should, to my mind, be seen as secondary to the picture itself.

Even that picture is, itself, a mixture of historical information and interpreting reflection. Already by the end of the first century, when most of the New Testament had been written, there was much which went far beyond what one could claim for the historical Jesus. And some claims have become very misleading. Yet careful examination of the earliest traditions about Jesus reveal enough information for us to be able to identify the contours of the Jesus behind it all. I want to say more about that in the next chapter about the Bible. It is our major source book for the picture of Jesus we have.

ooo

Jason

The cart was piled high with sacks of wheat. Jason made the journey every year, across the mountains to the valley of Poverty. The donkey was now quite old as it pulled the load the last steps of the way up into the city. The famine was severe. The relief had come almost too late.

The men and women who still had some strength welcomed him as a god. They had learned of his generosity from their parents. He brought life and hope. They helped him offload the sacks of wheat into the storehouse ready for distribution. No sooner was the tray empty than Jason bade them farewell and turned for the homeward journey.

Out through the city gate, past the parched fields, into the hill country and up the steep slopes of the first mountain pass. But this time it was different. The men

31

and women who had greeted him did not return his farewell cry. Instead they followed. They had learned to love this man and honour him.

When he stopped to rest at the brow of a hill, he looked back and there they were. As they approached, he beckoned to them to return. They fell to their knees. When they looked up at him, some thought they saw a golden glow which emanated from his face. The love he lived was radiant. 'He is God's own Son,' they whispered.

Jason turned away, for the journey was long and arduous and it was getting late. But again when he paused, they were soon there. They adored him. Some brought him gifts. Some took the gold rings from their fingers, others, items of jewelry and precious wood carvings. But before they could place them in his cart, Jason waved them back and continued his journey.

Late that evening he stopped once more and soon his followers were there again. The journey had excited them. They had had time to share wonderful stories about Jason, to make up songs which praised his generosity. They knew they had been visited by a god.

This time, as they again approached Jason's donkey and cart, suddenly a child appeared on horseback, riding from the village, pale faced, weakly and scarcely able to hold the mount. He rode up to Jason. The crowd gathered around. What had happened?

'They have died,' he said. 'Mother, father, the people in our street, the people over the way. All those who hungered in the village have died; only a few groan and gasp. I could not carry the wheat. There was no one to help. Those who were strong went off to follow after you...'

With that he collapsed to the ground. The followers surrounded his body. Gently one untied his shawl, slipping it from his shoulders. Others did the same, taking his tunic and undergarments, until the young man lay naked on the ground.

Jason wept. He was angry. 'Go back!' he called to them. 'Go back to the valley of Poverty! Go back for the people's sake! I shall come again.' Then he lifted the body onto the tray of his cart and continued on his way. At first the crowd was silent. 'Jason has failed us,' one whispered. 'No,' said another. 'Jason is God's Son. God's Son cannot fail.' By this time Jason was far away. Night had fallen. They made their way back in darkness.

---

ooo

What about the Bible?

Dear Kim

You have probably heard all kinds of things said about the Bible. What is it really? Let me begin by picking up where I left off in talking about Jesus.

The Bible is a major source of information about Jesus. This is because it contains, in the New Testament, a collection of writings from the first hundred years of Christianity. Among these writings are the four gospels which preserve for us many of the teachings of Jesus and a lot about what he did. Mostly they concentrate on the period in Jesus' life when he went about as a teacher, the last year or so of his life.

One of the reasons why people wrote the gospels is that those who knew Jesus directly were dying out and there was a real need to preserve an account of what Jesus said and did. But they were written quite late in the piece, after the Church had been in existence already for 40 or 50 years. This means they are a mixture of what Jesus may have originally said or done, mostly in the form of helpful anecdotes, and what people thought he might have said or done. People seem at many points to have added detail or occasionally trimmed it, in order to make things clearer or to bring out what they saw was the important point.

The gospels

Three of the gospels, Matthew, Mark and Luke, are very similar in detail. It looks as though Mark was written first, around 70 AD. Matthew and Luke independently reworked Mark's version of the events about 10 to 15 years later, adding in more material that had come to hand and rearranging the material. By the way they reworked Mark's story we can see the kinds of changes and additions which were probably made over the 40 years before Mark was written. It is not hard to imagine how, during this period, people shortened stories or collected sayings with similar themes or added brief comments to help people understand what was said.

So that is what the gospels are: collections of memories about Jesus made by the second and third generations of Christians. They don't claim to be anything more than that. That was enough, because the material they contain gives us a good impression of the kind of thing Jesus taught and what he did. Even when we sometimes cannot be really sure whether Jesus said this or that, or whether it was something the Church thought he said, it doesn't really matter, because it has all been produced under the impact of Jesus's influence. His impression has left its mark on the material and from that impression we can get a fairly good idea of what Jesus was like. That is why I have been quite confident in the last chapter in drawing the picture I have drawn.

We can find this impression of Jesus also in the other writings. The fourth gospel, John, is different from the others in being written more like a drama, with a lot of freedom in describing events and creating the conversation pieces. Jesus speaks in the language of the Church and makes direct claims for himself, which are really the claims which the Church of the time was making for him rather than anything he actually said. But, for that reason, people have often found it the most powerful gospel in putting in a nutshell who Jesus is. If people have a deep hunger for life's meaning, Jesus is 'the bread of life'; if people thirst for life, Jesus gives 'the water of life'. These are typical of the way the fourth gospel sets before us Jesus as the answer to our big questions about life and God.

The letters

The earliest Christian writings we have are the letters which Paul wrote. He had started up Christian communities in many of the major cities of Asia Minor (modern day Turkey) and Greece. He couldn't be everywhere at once and took to writing letters to keep in touch with them and to deal with local problems which had arisen. Fortunately we have a number of these letters. They are all fairly practical, dealing with issues as they came up. They allow us to see how he understood the Christian faith in the 50s, only some 20 years after Jesus' death. They are therefore particularly valuable in preserving how people thought about Jesus in earlier times and in adding to our impression of what Jesus must have been like.

Other New Testament writings include further letters of this kind from later times, some of them looking more like sermons sent to be read with a few greetings attached. Many were written in the name of one of the important leaders of the early church, like Peter or Paul, though not directly written by these leaders, themselves. Apart from that, we have Luke's second volume to his gospel, the Acts of the Apostles, which tells the history of the early church in its first 40 years, and the Book of Revelation.

The Book of Revelation is a collection of visions, full of symbols and codes which have fascinated people for centuries. We now know that the strange codes and symbols relate to the Roman Empire in the first century and were a way that one Christian writer tried to help local Christian communities cope with Roman oppression. Some of the images it uses are wierd. Unfortunately, people who do not know its historical background treat it as though it is a prophecy of world events of their own times. It has become the happy hunting ground of fanatical religious groups. It is not referring to Russia or China or Iraq or the Pope or the modern banking system, as various of these groups have suggested! Reading it in its own terms and its own time, you can see how inappropriate all this is. Yet its stark images still have something to say wherever political powers act oppressively against minorities and flout God's priorities.

The New Testament is the precious collection of early Christian writings. They came together partly because people valued them and made many copies of them and partly because later Church Councils set them apart as the authoritative selection for purposes of defining authentic Christianity. This had happened by the beginning of the fifth century.

The Old Testament

The larger collection of writings in the Bible is the Old Testament. It consists of writings of old Israel preserved by the Jewish people. It contains the major stories from their history which they looked to for their identity and where they encountered God. It also has much legal material, including detailed instructions of how the temple system was to run. Some of its most exciting material is in the writings of the prophets, who were kind of freelance preachers who used to challenge political and religious leaders of the community on matters of justice and truth, often in the face of great personal danger.

There are also collections of proverbs, poetry and shorter popular stories and the large psalm collection used in Israel's worship. Right at the beginning of the Bible we find a series of well known stories: the making of the world and of people (two different versions); Adam and

Eve; Cain and Abel; Noah's ark; and the Tower of Babel. These are similar to many of the ancient myths of the peoples of the region and should be treated as such, and not as historical, let alone scientific description. Yet they have a special quality, for they have been retold with significant modifications to bring out deep insights into human life and God.

Take the story of the tower of Babel, for example. It tells of people wanting to make a tower which would reach up into the heavens. Those in the heavens reply by destroying the tower and from that day people were scattered all over the earth with different languages. We can just imagine a little child asking, 'Why do people speak so many different languages?' and a parent telling the story. Yet at a deeper level this ancient myth alerts us to the tragedy which occurs when people overreach themselves and try to make a name for themselves, how it can bring division and lead to breakdown of communication and relationships. This is its message in the scriptures, not a theory about languages. Often we get the truth about life best from stories that are not necessarily true in the literal or historical sense.

Written by human hands

All of these writings were written by human beings in particular circumstances. They reflect those circumstances and the world view of their time. Naturally there is a lot of variety within the collections in quality and style. Some accounts of history are more valuable than others. Some preserve deeper insights than others. This is only to be expected of a collection of writings coming from almost a thousand year time span.

Even within the New Testament, where the time span is less than 100 years, there is considerable variety. With four different account of Jesus' life, there are inevitably quite different slants on some events and some contradictions in detail. Overall such things did not matter; what mattered, as far as the New Testament was concerned, was that this collection is our only major resource for what Jesus was like and the kind of impression he made on his followers. Who and what Jesus was, rubbed off on these people. Their writings allow us to sense something of the impact of who he was and what he did.

With the Old Testament it is similar. It is the body of writings belonging to a particular culture, Jewish culture, but Christians have always seen in these writings and in the history which they recount a place where the God-light has shone through in human affairs. In this regard its writings are quite mixed. There are awful stories of cruelty and massacre which their authors thought were willed by God. But there are also moments of tenderness and human love, challenges about social injustice and profoundly sensitive descriptions of what it means to live with pain. There is something of God captured or reflected in these writings which rings true to the picture we get of God through Jesus. But it is there in the mix typical of such a collection. To try to cut out the offensive nationalism of some parts or to try to distill only the purist thoughts would be a hopeless endeavour.

The same is true, ultimately, of the Bible as a whole. It is a human book by human authors written in very human situations in very human ways. Yet it is precisely as it is, that it has been a source of inspiration to so many down through the ages. It is a place where people have seen the light shining, have heard God speaking, have found their lives opened up in a new way.

For me, reading the Bible or hearing it discussed is like walking in a familiar garden. As a biblical scholar, I know most of the plants quite well. Some parts I don't find attractive. Here and there, there has been too much hacking about, when people have tried to straighten things out. Some of the beds look too much like they have been fitted into the going fashions. But at other points I just stand in wonder and it's as though I see things for the first time. It is always deeply rewarding to be in one of those 'God moments' that the Bible can make possible.

The Holy Bible and fundamentalism

You will see from what I have said that I am quite comfortable with seeing the Bible as it is and that I don't feel I have to pretend it is something else. I used to believe that Christians should see the Bible as absolutely perfect, without error, as God's own words and that to be critical of any part of it would be a terrible sin. Having come to know it in its historical setting and to see it as it is, I think I have a deeper, more profound reverence for it than I had before. It is holy because it has a unique role in preserving and opening up an encounter with Jesus and so with God. But for me it can do that without my having to pretend it is free of contradiction or offensive parts.

One of the most unfortunate things which has happened in many parts of Christianity is that people have gone overboard in their enthusiasm for the Bible and have ended up making false claims about it which do more harm than good to what it is on about. I say: it is the garden where I encounter God; I could use other words like: God speaks through it. When some people use the shorthand expression, 'the Word of God' for the Bible, they mean what I mean here, though I think the term has become so misleading I would prefer not to use it.

But if, instead of staying with revering God, I then go on and start revering the book, I could very easily end up claiming the Bible is somehow not human but divine. I would be more inclined to do this, the less I knew of its origin. So I could easily find myself claiming this is 'the Word of God' and mean something like: God controlled what the people wrote; it is completely without error and contradiction; it is permanently valid in every thought and rule it utters, quite independent of when the rule was written, by whom and for whom. This approach is commonly called fundamentalism and the same sort of thing is to be found in most religions, when people declare old traditions to be final, unchangeable, infallible authority.

I used to believe in the Bible in this way. People taught me that this was the only way to read the Bible and I believed them. For a while I tried to persuade everyone else this was so. In many ways it was simpler to ask people to believe everything the Bible said than to suggest it was complicated, with some things to be believed and some not. It also gave me a good feeling to believe I had the answers to everything, right there in the Bible. I shudder now at how arrogant and foolish I was, though I was very sincere and serious about it all.

It produced in me a narrow and inflexible attitude about what was right and wrong and about what people should believe. And I firmly believed I was right. When people believe like this and as long as they remain fixed in their attitude to the Bible, it can be like beating your head against a brick wall if you try to suggest alternative ways of looking at things. Many of the groups that go knocking on street doors are like this and so are many Christian groups today. I think I have a good understanding of what it is like to believe like this and to be so convinced.

When I reflect on it now, I can see that I held so intensely to such views not only because I thought they were right, but also because I was afraid of the alternatives. It seemed to me at the time that anything other than believing every word of the Bible was an offense to God and would destroy my faith. I can remember that the thing that changed my mind was not so much someone's arguments as someone's example. I began to see that there were people who believed differently from me whose lives were full of love and caring. Underneath I began to realise that I need not fear exploring other ways. There were real caring Christian who were not fundamentalists. I did not have to stay rigid and closed on the issue.

Freedom from fundamentalism

Later I realised that it was just this kind of rigid attitude towards religion and the Bible that Jesus and, later, Paul had to confront. Without realising it, I had been more on the side of Jesus' opponents than on the side of Jesus. The Bible, the Old Testament, as it was in Jesus' day, was quite unambiguous in much of what it asked people to do. For instance, if notorious sinners changed their ways, they were to follow a clearly set out procedure of going to the temple and making restitution before being received back into the community. Jesus seems to have short cut such arrangements and incurred the anger of the fundamentalist Pharisees; he offered them acceptance and forgiveness without such requirements.

In Paul's day the Church had to decide whether it was going to admit non-Jews into the Christian community. The first Christian were Jews. The Jewish scripture, the Old Testament, lays down procedures which non-Jews should follow if they want to join the community of God's people. It entailed going through a ritual which included circumcision of males, the cutting of loose skin from the end of the penis. In the name of openness and compassion Paul and his colleagues gave up the scripture command. Clearly they were operating on a different basis from the Bible-believing fundamentalists of the day. They were operating and living on the basis of the compassion that is at the heart of the biblical writings, not on the basis of the letter of its rules and regulations. Already then there were Christian fundamentalists who could only see such flexibility as an offense against God.

What emerged therefore was that some people were more concerned with rules and laws than they were with people. And, what is more, they represented God as more concerned with rules than with people. There is no doubt about their sincerity and devotion, but I see it as grossly misguided. Behind the two approaches are two different understandings of God. One pictures God as almost obsessed with getting people to do things 'his' way, like an egotistical person, pathetically self-preoccupied with his own power - a 'god' indeed! The other pictures God as compassionately reaching out to people making space for them, encouraging them and challenging them, wanting, above all, their wholeness. This picture of God also has room for guidelines and rules, but they exist for the sake of people and can be changed where a more compassionate option opens for us.

The danger of fundamentalism

This is the real danger of fundamentalism. It operates with a self obsessive image of God. Love takes second place to law; people take second place to rules. By contrast, Jesus shows the opposite stance when he declares: 'the sabbath was made for people, not people for the sabbath.' The fundamentalist approach has to take over into the modern era all the rules it finds in the biblical writings without modification. There can be no allowances made for change of culture or growth in understanding. In the later chapter on 'Right and Wrong' you will see how the fundamentalist approach tends to present a rigidly cruel response to a wide range of issues, from divorce and remarriage to homosexuality and the role of women.

The issue is confused, however, because most fundamentalists are not consistent. The same arguments they use to oppose equality of women should, strictly speaking, also lead them to oppose the abolition of slavery, to oppose women attending worship with heads uncovered, to oppose the banking system, because Bible texts can be found which oppose each of these. Yet among fundamentalists there is rarely a thoroughgoing consistency. On some questions, for instance, people will have no qualms dropping some scripture requirements, such as those which calls for slaves to obey masters or those forbidding divorce.

But frequently they also add other rules, like abstention from alcohol, or, in earlier days, from dancing, gambling, card playing, cinema. When I consider the way I used to think as a fundamentalist, I can see now that it was really a mixture of fundamentalism with particular cultural values thrown in which had, in fact, very little to do with the Bible.

I often see fundamentalists caught between their loyalty to the Bible as they understand it and compassion for people; but they are not free to choose love as long as they bind themselves to their understanding of the Bible. Or their compassion can operate only within certain set limits. That is very sad and the opposite of what the Bible is ultimately about.

I shall return to some of the above issues in the chapter on 'Right and Wrong,' The main point I am making here is that I think it is essential that we free ourselves from the kind of fundamentalism which I have described, in order to be free to be in line with what the Bible is all about: becoming part of God's loving in the world. This is an uphill battle, because so many people fear that to depart from this attitude to the Bible is a terrible sin. If only they could see that it is a far greater sin to stay with it and cut oneself and others off from the freedom to respond with love and compassion to one's fellow human beings.

Walking in the garden

If we are to approach the Bible as the precious collection of writings that it is and walk in its garden, how do we do this? One simple way is to pick up the Bible and read it, starting from the beginning or starting with a gospel. Using a good flowing English translation you can read large chunks at a time. Another way is to read it in small segments, using an aid to understanding like, 'With Love to the World', which gives half a page comment for each day's reading. I think something like this is better, because many parts of the Bible are obscure and need further explanation to help us make a connection with what they are saying. It is also valuable because the selection of daily readings matches those set to be read on the following Sunday in many of the major Churches.

Probably the most natural way to enjoy the garden is to go there with other people. Most of the writings were written to be read aloud in a group of people where they could be appreciated and discussed and reflected upon. That can be even better than having a commentary. They are writings that come from a community and are best understood in a community. In the community you can find resources and information which throws light both on what the writings of the Bible meant and how they may throw light on questions and issues today.

In fact, meeting with people who are also sharing the same journey, trying to live in the light of what Jesus was saying about God, can be one of the most enriching experiences of life. That brings me to the Church which can sometimes be just that, but all too often is not.

A Reflection on Lent

The forty days of Lent, beginning with Ash Wednesday, prepare us for Good Friday and the Easter celebration. They are a time when we reflect on the meaning of our faith. They remind us of Jesus who spent 40 days in the wilderness preparing for his ministry.

The wilderness of Judea is a barren stretch of smooth rolling hill country. Almost nothing grows there. When I was there in summer, 1988, there was a faint tinge of yellow brown on the hillsides. That year had been an exception: there had been a patch of rain. I sometimes wonder: what if Jesus had spent 40 days in our West Australian wilderness, our bushland? I invite you to come exploring as we imagine what Jesus might see...

The bull ants on the track seem almost to outrun us as we walk along. The kangaroo droppings at the side say there is life here; but none is to be seen. The sand tells a story: here a bobtail crossed; there a rabbit; and over here we see the trail of a snake's winding path. Our wilderness is full, brimming with signs, but dry - parched. We cannot stay here long; there is no water. We do not know the secrets of the small shrubs who defiantly display their green to the scorching sun and in season charm the insects with their colours.

It is a rich wilderness, barren, but full of adventure. Not far away motor cars scream past on the highway in search of gold and ambition, while just metres from the road a treasury awaits those who stop still, take measured steps, and pause to listen to the tiny wonders which chime their beauty through the crusted earth. These would be the angels that would minister to him, God's messengers in the sunshine, earth's tenderness unfolding life, each a new creation, a new possibility seen or unseen.

This is a bed of prayer, a tranquility one can smell, the incense of the eucalypts forever moist, the recitations and chants of small honey eaters, the shouting hallelujahs of wattle birds, the sonorous groan of the black crow. This is a holy land, a place of preparation.

But others have been here before us. The majestic black boys, erect and branching, pointing to the sky, stand among others smashed, their bodies strewn like small piano keys upon the sand. What violence is this? What being can rip nature apart, tear its heart, violate its body. It sends a shudder down the spine. So many of its people decimated - above the shadows of brokenness there is still flowering: miracle!

This is a place of brokenness and hope. Antlers emerge on the skyline of trees now eaten out by white ants, half failed branches holding life and death aloft for all to see. Here gushes exuberant green, there leaves turned brown, and, within, a hollowed blackness all but swallowing the sap's rising, but not quite. The burning, the nothingness, the charred testimony to the cross writ across nature itself. Yet out of this astonishing pain small green resurrections assert themselves. Out of charred and cracked casks of death, seeds squeeze forth to begin again. The wild absurdity of death turned to life! Easter before our eyes!

The twenty-eight parrot, above, toots its signal as if to herald the new insight and, far off, the confused screeching and squawking of galahs, like an untrained choir, sound their assent. To be here is to find life. To stay here is to die. Here is the place of fantasy; there is a world full of Zacchaeus, full of the woman at the well, full of Pilate, full of religious people, full of blind men crying, Son of David. Here is the place of serenity and reflection, disturbed only by the persistence of the flies; there mountains will move, earth will shake and crowds will shout, 'Crucify!'

My toes sink into the warm sand. I have stood too long. Was I alone? Or was he really there, too? I can find my way back to the road. I can drive off along paved roads. I can return to plastered concrete buildings and white lines. I can merge again into the asphalt of the city. I can die according to the street plan. There is order there, no room for green shoots to crack the pavement. Not even a tinge of yellow brown if I choose death. Just solidarity with a paralysis that sprawls over the landscape and threatens to make the whole orb of earth grey - and there would be darkness over the whole earth from the sixth hour - forever. The leschenaultia tells me the true colour of the sky. The banksia is a lamp for my path. The purple hardenbergia leads me across the tangles of the undergrowth. The eucalypt refreshes my soul. The bottlebrush and grevillea provide beacons of celebration. The acacia is my rich treasure of gold. The blackboy is my original and Aboriginal guide pointing upwards to life. The cats paw is the little secret behind the bushes there for each one of us.

The ants are still running, but he has moved on. Now he stands by the broken tree. The black cockatoos wheel overhead and screech. Is it happening again? I wait and I wonder. Do I see what I see when I see?

ooo

What about the Church ?

Dear Kim

Church is boring! That's what I often hear people say and sometimes I feel like that, too. Something seems to have gone wrong. Yet it is not always what I feel. Sometimes I feel proud to be identified with the Church - when it stands up for human rights, when it gets involved in helping people who have real need, when it is a place which helps me get in touch with God in my life. I also know that some of my most important experiences have happened in church. So I have very mixed feelings about the Church.

Part of me feels very impatient with the Church and with what happens in it. I can get quite exasperated when people in the Church think that Christianity is all about being rigid and strict or when they trot out ideas about the faith that make it all seem like mumbo jumbo or like a club to make comfortable people feel more comfortable.

Yet some of the most exciting people I have met have been in the Church. They challenge me. They wake up my ideas. They seem to be in touch with life. They open up new ways of looking at things. They are generous, loving people, who illustrate by their lives everything I have been saying about Jesus. They are real saints. You probably know some people like that, too. They're not necessarily people in official Church positions; often they are not; some of them are. They are just people getting on with life, but with an abundance of love to give to others.

At other times, being in Church feels like being in a hospital, especially when I've got to know the people around me a little. Some sit there in the congregation, carrying recent memories of someone close to them who has died. Others come, full of worry and fear about their job or their health or what is happening to their kids or their marriage. Some seem to be regularly depressed people; and others are a bit odd and seem to feel at home here and few places else.

When the minister and those leading the worship are tuned in to where people are at, the whole event can seem like an act of healing. The whole room fills with compassion and you feel a close sense of belonging together - limping along with the lame, holding the hand of the elderly, putting your arm round the shoulders of someone going through rough times. And sometimes this can happen quite literally, especially where everything is not all stiff and starchy.

An odd mixture

The Church - any congregation - and the Church as a whole is an odd mixture, a strange assortment of people. Some of them are in the Church out of habit and tradition, without much commitment to what it is all about - in fact, often blocking any initiatives to be relevant to the world around us. Others are there by habit and tradition because they have always tried to walk the way of Jesus in their lives. They were there when it was what everyone used to do; they are there when it's out of fashion.

Then I wonder what it would have been like around Jesus in his day. There would probably have been a similar assortment of different people. Perhaps a number who presently go to church would be more comfortable with Jesus' opponents; but, all the same, you'd be in an uncomfortable crowd of people at all different stages of life's journey. It is tempting to think: wouldn't it be better if I could find a lot of people who think more or less the way I do? Sometimes I long for that; but then that seems like asking Jesus to be selective about his company.

In moments of truth I also realise that we're all people who are on a journey and I'm no exception. In some ways the progress Christianity has made in the world or in the Church is about the same as it has made in my own life - otherwise I'm kidding myself. And I'm not about to abandon myself; so I'm not going to abandon the Church just because it's as human as I am.

That sounds simpler than it really is. At least I can make some changes in myself; with the Church that's more difficult; will anyone listen? Part of loving myself as God loves me means looking at my faults and deciding to do something about them. I need to love the Church like that, too - I am also part of it! What I want to say about the Church comes from this approach. Let me begin with the great treasure that the Church is.

The wider Church

The Church is the local congregation; but it is also bigger than that. It is worldwide and it reaches back across nearly 2000 years. When I'm in Church, I sense quite strongly at times this link with the whole wider Church. Sometimes people leading the worship help to engender this sense by pointing it out or using it in some way. Sometimes we pray or talk about people outside our own local Church. That's the horizontal aspect: the Church across all the peoples and cultures of today's world. The vertical aspect is the one which makes me feel one with Christians down through the ages, right back to the first disciples and Jesus himself. The traditional way of saying what I am treasuring here is that the Church is the one, holy, catholic and apostolic Church. 'Catholic', here, is used in its archaic sense of 'universal'. 'Apostolic' means it goes back to the apostles, the first Christian leaders.

In tune with yesterday - and today?

Treasuring the connection with all those who have been Christians in the Church over the centuries is why I'm comfortable about using ancient prayers or creeds and hymns at times in church. But they shouldn't, to my mind, dominate and leave no room for saying and doing things in today's ways as well. That's a problem in Church services. Some use only traditional sources. That can be fine for those who are in the in-group. I think too many churches have got stuck with only one kind of tradition in words and in music. They don't seem to realise that they are giving people the message that what they are about can't really be celebrated or lived in today's world. I know they wouldn't see what they are doing as defeatist nostalgia, but I suspect it is often close to it. At worst it is a form of community depression.

Sometimes the opposite happens and I find it very odd. You can have modern swinging music used with words that are anything but modern. There are a lot of very sloppy words around for choruses and they mostly come from churches where all the emphasis seems to be on my feeling happy inside. When I take services in congregations which use one of these popular collections, I usually have enormous difficulty finding songs which are about God's love reaching out into practical areas of life or about social justice. It's usually all very soapy self-indulgent stuff. One of the funniest things I have noticed in many congregations I have visited which use choruses is that, when they do have traditional hymns, the organists play them so slowly it is like singing a dirge!

But I will still use these collections, because not all of the choruses are of the shallow kind and I have yet to find alternative resources. I long for the input which creative musicians with a sensitive tolerance to a wide range of musical style could make to the Church. I'm a classical music fan, myself, but I can't, for the life of me, justify the monoculturalism which dominates among those who seem to make the decisions about

48

the music of the Church and the words and style of its written orders of service. There is a kind of stuck-ness here which belongs to a wider problem in the Churches.

Fundamentalism also about the Church

The general stuck-ness in the Church is almost a kind of fundamentalism; only, instead of treating the Bible as divine and infallible, people have treated the Church and its institutions as infallible. We treasure the Bible as our earliest witness to God in history, but some couldn't help going on to make the Bible, itself, divine. At its worst, we have a similar phenomenon in the Church, where some people treat the way the Church has been organised from the second century onwards as somehow sacrosanct, as divine. That means: nothing is to be changed!

This rather odd tendency to go too far in devotion also explains how some Catholics came to treat Mass (Holy Communion) as something almost magical and to revere the Pope as infallible. We can almost see the same steps occurring: I have a profound sense of Jesus' presence at Communion and jump to the conclusion that Communion must enshrine a magical act that makes the bread and wine quite literally the physical body and blood of Jesus. Or, I believe God speaks through the Pope and jump to the conclusion that everything he says must be infallible. More informed Catholics would explain to us that neither of these views truly represents Catholic doctrine. But they are typical of a tendency we have already noted with regard to the Bible and which, we have seen, also affects some people's attitude to the institutions of the Church.

These more extreme positions about the Church become all the more absurd when people justify them by claiming that Jesus set the Church up in this way, whereas we now know quite well that the organisation of the Church evolved in response to purely pragmatic concerns over a long period of time. The pragmatic concerns of the Church's mission of love still need to be the ultimate criterion for deciding how we should organise our lives in the Church.

In its less extreme form we find this kind of fundamentalism about the Church in the great fear and reluctance which people, including many clergy, have, about doing different, more imaginative things in the areas of music, worship activity and about finding more imaginitive and effective ways of being the Church in the world.

How much do we hold on to?

But there is another side to the coin and it explains why the Church has often found itself stuck and not able to move. It relates to what I was saying about a sense of belonging with those who have gone before us. Saying the creeds, using parts of the ancient liturgy of Holy Communion and singing ancient hymns all help us sense that we belong to that great historic community of faith. The question is: how much do we hold onto in order to retain that connection? Congregations where all such links with the past have been ignored (except the Bible) seem to me to be greatly impoverished.

The Bible is our key link with the earliest days of the Christian Church. But there are other important links. These include the service of Holy Communion which in most churches still retains ancient prayers like: 'Holy, holy, holy Lord..' or 'Lamb of God, you take away the sin of the world,..' and a number of others. The basic forms of the Holy Communion Service and of Baptism, including Baptism of infants, reach right back to the time even before the Bible received its final stamp of approval.

Ministries

Another important link which people include is having people set aside (ordained) as ministers to help the Church to keep a good hold on its connections with the ancient Church, especially the Bible, and to reflect on the impact these can have on present day living. The more ancient branches of the Church argue that we should preserve not only the ordained ministry but also the way the Church structured its ordained ministry from the second century onwards. That structure had three kinds of minister: bishops, priests and deacons. 'Bishops' originally meant 'overseers'. 'Priests' replaced the term 'elders' in the second century and means the minister of the local congregation. 'Deacons' was, and still is, a rather loose term which can range from meaning ministers with a special focus on social work and caring functions through to little more than apprentice priests. Most Churches recognise that these forms of ministry cover some of the key functions every church must have in its ministry, but some continue to insist, more literally, on having precisely these forms of ministry and using precisely these words, bishops, priests and deacons, even though, in reality, they are now very different from what they were in the second century.

Standing in the stream

There is much more that some would add to the list of what should be preserved unchanged. The power and wonder of the message of the gospel of love inevitably resulted in magnificent art and music and a myriad of traditional practices and rites which came to carry special meaning for people. People of one culture or one Church denomination developed their own particular traits. The Church in its history has given the world wonderful treasures, magnificent architecture, beautiful music. Each Church and each culture has found its own way of being the Church and of seeking to serve as a channel of the impact of Jesus.

If you stand in the stream of the Christian gospel today, you stand in a stream which has flowed through many of these channels. It is in many ways a beautiful heritage. We cannot change that even if we wanted to. It is given to us. But how do we live as a body of Christians today? Some will want to enter fully into the marvels of that inheritance and will find it inspires them for living out the gospel in fresh ways today. Others will know little of it and not find it greatly inspiring. That is our choice. People are different and to some extent different denominations reflect such options much more than they do profound differences in belief.

But the question is, when is it a matter of choice and when does it become a matter of obligation? When is it a matter of recognising people's rights to different cultural expressions of the gospel and when is it a matter of holding onto something without which Christianity ceases to be Christianity? Putting it in this way makes us face the issue: what is it in Christianity that we want to preserve?

I myself would want to put the ancient formats of Holy Communion and of Church organization, including ordination to a threefold ministry as commonly defined, in the optional category. I want to keep Holy Communion central, though I can conceive of what is essential to Christianity without it (as in the Salvation Army). Further, I believe we need order and organization in structuring the Church's life. At least we need to be exercising the functions represented in the so-called historic patterns of ministry. But even in saying this I am aware I am being very traditional and adapting myself to what is familiar.

I suspect the Church is too 'hung up' in all these matters and is too much concerned with preserving what has been deemed authoritative and is less free for celebration and service appropriate to current need than it ought to be. It was because Jesus shortcut the established procedures for ordering community life to meet the immediate needs of people that he came into conflict with his religious contemporaries. More than once I have felt myself on the wrong side of this conflict. It seems to me, for instance, that anything other than an open table at Holy Communion where all may feed puts us on the side of Jesus' critics. Yet most churches still impose limitations.

Obsessions of religious people

It is my view that what we see as the obsessions of the religious people of Jesus' day are not so different from what have become the obsessions of many in the Church. They mostly touch situations where allegedly divinely sanctioned law and ordinance are given higher priority than human need. The Church too often finds itself not on the side of flexibility. There is a quasi fundamentalism often operating in discussions of such matters as church order, ordination of women, divorce and remarriage, and who may receive or celebrate Holy Communion.

At worst, we find ourselves back with a puny understanding of God, who is liable to get terribly upset if things are not done in exactly the right way, the way they have always been done. I sometimes think our images of God are blasphemously sick. Would any of us, at our best, behave the way God is, at times, alleged to behave? God is assumed to be so rigidly tied up in rules and to be completely bereft of flexibility. Parents, at their best, encourage children to experiment, to ask questions and to explore and they stay with them even when they have their doubts. I can't believe any less of God; yet so often the picture I get is of a very insecure God, with little trust and full of oppressive fear. This is not the God I find in Jesus.

Setting boundaries and keeping our identity

To stay with the image of parenting, parents also need to know the importance of setting boundaries. Many of the Church's traditions have arisen from just such a need. The need continues. Within the community of faith we need to recognise that we are not perfect; there are things we do not see; we make mistakes. We need each other and we need the voices of the past. They are brought to us through tradition, especially in its earliest form, the scriptures. We also need to listen to the skilled interpreters of Bible and tradition and to those in the present whom we recognise as especially wise.

I am all for our having a very positive, appreciative attitude towards what has gone before us in the stream and a respect for the various practices which have become special to people. However I think that this can all happen without losing sight of the first priority, living out the good news about God we find in Jesus in the present. I am not advocating that the Church abandon its tradition - Jesus was not advocating that to the religious leaders of his day; but he was calling them back to what really mattered and he sat lightly, when necessary, to the rest. I think the Church needs to live by that principle.

You and me and the Church

Where does that leave you and me, as individuals, in relationship to the Church? As I said, I think each of us as individuals faces similar issues in our own lives to those faced by the Church. We need to show the Church community the same tolerance. For instance, there are plenty of people who, in a similar way to the Church, get stuck with doing things the way they have always done them and who do not seem to have the flexibility to make changes that would be so good for them and for those around them. That doesn't mean forgetting everything we were. We can't do that; but being alive means being awake to doing things in new ways as new situations arise and to following old patterns only when they are still relevant.

A way of being together?

How, then, do I, as an individual, relate to the Church? I go along to Church and sometimes to wider Church gatherings and I meet all the things I have just described. I feel I belong there, even when I feel frustrated and it is hard. I will continue to go. But I know I also need more than that. I also value the support, encouragement and friendship from others who are on the same path of faith. I value plain talking and direct personal encounter, meeting people and being enriched by sharing issues and experiences with them. Therefore I need to be able to get closer to people than ever I could in a large (or small) Sunday congregation.

I don't want to give up the rest and stay only with a close or closed group, though I know a lot of people who have chosen this path and I have a lot of sympathy with them. In fact, my hunch is that many people are outside the Church today because nothing like this existed for them within the Christian community. It is asking a lot of people to expect them to come each Sunday to a traditional service and there decode, demythologise, and translate what is going on before they can gain any benefit from it - it can be hard work! I sometimes find it so. We are losing, or have already lost, many of our more thinking and more feeling souls by our persistence in pandering to more staid and conservative movements in the Church and the fear they engender, especially among clergy wanting to feel accepted. In the smaller more intimate group there would be a place for such people (and for me!).

In this respect I often find it strange that few people reflect on the major changes which came about in Christianity when, after flourishing successfully for two hundred years, it finally received authority to build churches, that is, church buildings. Before that Christians met in houses. Groups must have been smaller than most of our congregations. The house would add greater intimacy and informality. The Communion would probably have been served from the meal table and usually after or in connection with a normal meal. They still had sermons, at least, according to Acts, because there is the celebrated incident of someone going to sleep and falling out a window!

In some cities there were a number of such house churches. We don't know whether, or how often, they would have all crammed together for a common celebration or service. Probably they did from time to time. It seems to me that such a system had special value worth recovering. I sometimes have a vision of Christians returning to make the local house group their main gathering and feeding centre again and meeting only, say, once a month in the wider group.

As I've said above, I think the wider connection with other Christians is essential and I sometimes find it very uplifting, but I wonder if making Christianity's main activity a weekly Sunday meeting in a large hall or specially constructed building has not robbed Christianity of something vital. I hope we will see more experiments in this direction. It would have immediate implications for our traditional understanding of ordained ministry and administration of the sacraments, but this would be a refreshing change. It would also call for ministers to play a major support role for group leaders.

The danger I would see in such groups, apart from the possibility of poor resourcing and oversight, is potential exclusiveness. We would need to make all sorts welcome in our homes and learn to live with much greater openness, abandoning the 'my little castle' approach to own homes. Maybe that, in itself, would make us more Christian where it counts - in the neighbourhood! A feature of earliest Christianity, soon noted by outsiders, was its hospitality.

In my imagining I still see a role for the local congregation, groups for the children, youth and adults, and occasions of worship and celebration. I hope the churches will continue to be centres of vibrant life for young families in the new suburbs. Coming to a friendly congregation where the children have something for them and you find something for yourself can be an enrichment and inspiration for the week. Appropriate worship and fellowship for seniors in the older centres of population must continue to be a strong feature. It's everyone in between that worries me and where I think we need greater flexibility and more imagination. The worsening financial state of the Church will probably force the Church to consider some of these options, but it would be far better if they were looked at with a view to being more effective than only with a view to saving money.

The extraordinary achievements of local churches

For someone like myself, involved personally and professionally in the Church, it is easy to touch on the sore spots in the Church and also to have blind spots. I also need to remind myself of the extraordinary achievements of the Church in so many unsung ways. Often no one knows the comfort, help and healing given by so many clergy and lay visitors to families facing grief. Few hear of the hours of support of people in crisis in the their relationships or within themselves. Ministers and priests are still among the few helpers who feel comfortable, or for whom it is socially acceptable, to make initiating house calls. Much of the front line caring in this way goes unnoticed as people are helped to stand on their own feet again or are referred to helping agencies.

In some congregations there are elaborate networks of mutual caring and support which spill over into the surrounding neighbourhood; few notice the delivered casserole on the doorstep; and the conversation over morning tea at breaking point remains confidential. There is often a privacy about the visit on the anniversary of the death of a spouse or loved one and only the proud and patronising will want to report to all and sundry about relief and assistance brought to the unemployed family or new immigrants.

Church knockers are frequently ignorant of the life given lonely youth in the local church club or by the parents of one teenager to another who just had to spill it all out, because she couldn't approach her own parents. The fellowship which many with disabilities find in church groups or the shelter found by the homeless kids do not make headlines, except in the occasional excesses of some parachurch groups seeking public funds.

Newspapers prefer to report problems and the lashings out by oppressed cultural and ethnic groups than to focus on their creative forms of Christian community which are bringing hope and new vision to so many. Occasionally the Church makes its voice heard on matters of poverty, discrimination and injustice; but its more progressive forms have constantly been out front in challenging the dehumanising forces of exploitation which frequently hide behind Christian respectability. From the church have come many of the courageous heroes of communism's collapse in the east, of apartheid's dismantling, of movements for justice within our own countries, of the growth of the peace movement and of the establishment in public consciousness of the need to conserve the environment.

A holy place built of people

The Church continues to be for so many a place where they find inner stillness and peace, a holy place or a gathering of people which treasures and fosters the sense of awe and wonder that is the essence of worship. I like the image of the church as a community of people being like a building put together from rocks and stones of all various shapes and sizes, some smooth and hard, some weathered and broken, some beautiful, some very plain, some soft or brittle, some very old, some very young, but all together creating a place where people can sense and enjoy the presence of God. There's room for everyone and for all sorts.

It is, therefore, out of the Church, this mixed bag of humanity, with all its warts and disfigurements, that, nevertheless, something beautiful has been possible that goes beyond the ugliness of which it has also been capable. I have this faith in the Church that the stream still flows and that, as long as it does, the life will be there and the love that matters will break through. At times as I stand in the stream I notice an awful lot of sludge and rubbish passing me by; but the same stream also channels life giving nutrient. It is worth being there.

I believe the Church still has good water to offer. In parts it urgently needs to clean up its banks and to make its waters more accessible. But the water is there, the same water that has quenched people's deep inner thirst for two thousand years and brought parched desert places of humanity to the miracles of peace and love. I believe, too, that that good water also helps us face issues of Right and Wrong to which we address ourselves in the following chapter.

A hundred thousand dollars!

a reflection on Luke 12:13-21

A hundred thousand dollars!
Yes, if I transfer the mortgage to the other side of the
  ledger,
put my existence into recess for a year on full salary,
sell up my assets,
take my library to the cash converters,
I could have a hundred thousand dollars!

A hundred thousand dollars!
A hundred thousand years, she said;
A hundred and twenty thousand years.
Little fragments of bone looking up out of the sand,
smiling, weeping, witnesses to a black history,
discovered by the archaeologist,
delighting the anthopologist,
astounding the ethnologist,
lucky not to be caught up in the scoop
to join others now encased in the concrete mix
that holds aloft walls of city barns
or hangs heavy over mother earth
beneath the trampling of the feet.

A hundred thousand dollars!
A hundred and forty four thousand virgins,
men and women who shunned the unholy alliance
  with Babylon,
clothed in garments bloodied by solidarity with the
  saviour
and those he came to save.
Rich in their poverty,
glorious in their humility,
an alternative people,
uncomfortable with centuries of religious patronage
of the prevailing culture
and the blessing of those who win.

A hundred thousand dollars and bigger barns!
Barns of knowing and more knowing,

power and more power,
buzzing with technology,
systems retrieval, retrieval systems, systems retrieval,
possessing, cataloguing, analysing, expanding.
I have it, beyond pregnancy;
here there will be no child, just a knowing that ex-
    pands,
that encompasses more and more
until the barn itself envelops all reality
and outside is but wasteland;
and God is blown away in the wind.

A hundred thousand dollars!
Twenty pieces of silver, a lot less,
a different currency, but the same trade.
Jesus, you might have been high priest;
you might have founded a new movement in Judaism,
a new world organisation to control men's minds
and mediate to women and children grace possessed
and marketed through mystery and rite.
Judas, you succeeded.
If you did not force his hand,
you forced theirs and ours
and our heritage preserves the gold
only amid tarnished images.

A hundred thousand dollars!
When the train stopped, we ran across the icy potato
    fields;
the other refugees were too weak to move.
No Russians were there.
We could dig and scratch,
if lucky, finding beneath the cold crusted surface
potatoes left in the warmer earth below.
This was our food; there were no rations.
I clawed for my little child - two years old;
and for others, desperate on the flight from east to
    west.
Then someone found it, a half rotted case of sodden
    leather
but inside coins and notes,
a hundred thousand, a million and more,

a currency now rendered worthless by post war
    devaluation.
But in our hands it became light;
it became a new currency of compassion;
as in our fantasy we shared its wealth,
there was food and drink,
nourishment, relief, companionship,
a meeting of hope, hope to go on,
hope to hold on
as they shut the carriage doors again for the journey.

A hundred thousand dollars!
How can we adjust the budget?
Do recessions bottom out?
Pious romanticism won't pay wages.
There is no substitute for the challenge to give more.
So much depends on it. Let's not kid ourselves.
We need barns and we need to keep them up.
But what if the tide goes out?
Yes, we cannot swim, but have you discovered the
    rock pools?
Perhaps to walk the mudflats does more than dirty the
    feet.
Could a new church arise?
A mangrove church, unspectacular,
but sustaining of life in ways unseen and unknown.
Will some now trained return to fishing
and spend weekends finding crabs to share?
Give me a hundred thousand dollars today for the
    budget's sake!
But give me more the sense of beauty when the tide is
    out.

A hundred thousand dollars!
Now spilt on the floor,
running off Jesus' feet,
mixed with tears.
Oil and water don't mix.
How inappropriate.
It's all wrong.
That money could have been spent for the poor.
We needed it for our budget.

I need it for my mortgage!
A loose woman, still loose,
a loser, losing, still losing,
and strangely finding.

A hundred thousand dollars!
To feed five thousand.
Go on, Andrew,
McDonalds or Chicken Treat,
Kentucky Fried or Chinese takeaway.
Men and manna in the desert;
magic on the road,
unrepeatable in Ethiopia,
and then not even able to be delivered.
Repeatable on a world scale,
on every quaint communion table of bread and wine,
crafted to the culture of the years,
when men and women believe the magic and catch the
    vision.
Little girls and little boys with little loaves
living only for this.

A hundred thousand dollars!
A thousand, a hundred, ten, and one;
Me and you and us and them and all.
Receive the treasure, grace for everyone.

And know that barns and bigger barns will fall.

---

ooo

What about right and wrong ?

Dear Kim

Sex before marriage, abortion, masturbation, prostitution, gambling, alcohol, smoking, playing sport on Sundays, homosexuality, mercy killing, profiteering, embryo experimentation, drugs....there are lots of areas where we need to know what is right and wrong.

The Church has often been a place where people have expected answers. And often, especially in the past, some in the Church have given answers, even when people weren't asking questions. Worse still, they have been often quick to condemn people. Nobody likes 'holier than thou' types or people who seem to have all the answers. Jesus had his fair share of conflict with religious people of this kind. As we have seen, for him people mattered most and rules or guidelines were there to help people; people were not made to be fitted into someone else's rules and regulations - not even God's. God is much more generous than that!

But all the same, we do face decisions and the Church carries with it nearly 3000 years of wisdom on a wide range of issues. It's worth listening to what people found to be right in the past. But, for many people, that is only half the story; there is not only wisdom; there are absolute commandments given by God which must be obeyed. They are not to be questioned; they are only to be obeyed.

I have some problems with this, especially if it means that I am doing things in a kind of blind obedience. I may choose quite freely to obey a commandment given me in this way, but I would much prefer to choose to do it also because it seems right and good. Do I do it because I'm told to or do I do it because I believe it is right and good? I much prefer the latter; it is also how I see good parenting. There's a lot of difference between telling someone to do something 'because I say so!' and getting them to do it because it is right and good for them and for others. The second way shows far more respect for the person.

Love before laws, people before rules

Ultimately, it is respect for people, caring about others and oneself, in short, love, which lies at the heart of Jesus' picture of God. Everything, even creation itself, stems from God's goodness. I don't mind saying that there is one demand I do feel and that is God's demand of love. But, even so, to speak of love in this way, as God's demand, still makes it feel too narrow. It robs it of its life. Love is much more than a demand. It is wanting what is good. It is caring about others and the world.

So when I think about right and wrong, I don't start with a set of rules, not even a set of commandments, but with this central theme of love. But, as soon as I start looking at specific situations, I grasp for every bit of assistance I can get. Not that I don't trust my own ability to make a decision. But I know myself well enough to know that I can usually only see things in a limited way. I'm not God. Others will see things I don't see. This is one of the reasons why the more we can make decisions about right and wrong in discussion with others, the better. Also, if I am deciding on something where I am emotionally involved, there's an even greater chance that I may skew my own reasoning and neglect important things. This is also where the wisdom and the rules of previous generations become very helpful. But they need to be weighed up carefully.

Take a matter like divorce. There's little doubt that Jesus took a very strict line on divorce and forbad it. He must have felt this was really important in his social situation where divorce was being used against women and driving many of them to poverty. Perhaps he saw no other way.

It would be quite logical to apply the same law today and say that at least people wanting to be followers of Jesus should not divorce. How can you change a law laid down by Jesus? Yet many Christians and many Churches today have come to accept divorce as the more loving and creative solution to some marriage situations. Are they turning their back on Jesus? It depends how you see it. At one level they are; but at another level they are putting Jesus' message of love at the centre and acting on that basis. In many situations to abide by Jesus' divorce instruction would be to contradict the thrust of his central message. In such situations we follow Jesus more truly by being loving than we would by staying with rules.

What about sex?

What about sex before marriage and sex among people not or no longer married? The history of human thinking about sex is very complex. Most ancient religions have special rules about sex. Partly these are to prevent unwanted pregancies and to keep society stable by having children born into families where they can be cared for. Partly they have to do with the sense that sex brings people into close connection with major life and death issues. Menstruation, childbirth, male ejaculation, marriage were all seen to be connected with holy things and there were usually special rituals associated with each. There were many taboos connected with sex; possibly Paul's concern about women's head covering in Church goes back to an established taboo. In some ancient religions, at the same time, sexual intercourse, itself, was used as a sacred rite, a way to be in contact with the gods.

The Bible and sex

The people of Israel, whose attitudes are preserved in the Old Testament and strongly reflected in the New Testament, shared many of these understandings. In their earlier traditions they show that it was not uncommon for men to have more than one wife (not vice versa!) and to sleep with their slave women. Later we find having one wife was becoming the norm. On the negative side, they came to draw the line strictly at prostitution and at the use of sex as a religious rite. They were strict in forbidding sexual intercourse before and outside of marriage. And they also rejected all forms of homosexual practice, buggery (sex with animals), incest and rape.

By the time of Jesus and the New Testament the norm and rule was that sex belonged in marriage. In the world of New Testament times there was even a tendency among popular moral teachers, both Jewish and non Jewish, to play down sexual pleasure as an unworthy concern and to argue that sex should be engaged in primarily for the purpose of bringing children into the world. This was the noble way to live. In this respect it is, therefore, interesting that Paul did not conform to this trend. Although a bachelor himself and also sharing some of this reluctance about sexuality, Paul is happy to support those who, as he puts it, were 'burning' with sexual passion. He says that for them to go ahead and find fulfilment in marriage is a good thing. His view was obviously not as narrow as many of the moral teachers of his time.

On most questions of sexual morality the Bible is quite unambiguous. For some, especially fundamentalists, that settles the issue once and for all. People are still the same; the rules are still the same. But, quite apart from not wanting to treat the Bible in this way, I also believe that there have been some changes which mean we must look at many of these issues in a new way.

Has anything changed?

One major change is that human beings have discovered far more effective means of contraception. There need be no fear of unwanted pregnancies where contraceptives are available and effective. If such contraceptive capacity had been available in these ancient cultures, would their rules about sex before marriage have been different? I suspect they would have been. We are in a different situation and I no longer consider it appropriate to carry over into our own time without question such rules developed for a largely non-contraceptive society. We are the first generations living in a contraceptive society and I think we must make our own discoveries about boundary setting and do so, as far as possible, without the guilt and fear which has so often accompanied sex in our western society.

Are there any guidelines?

Does this mean we are now all at sea without any directions to help us? I don't think so. It was, after all, not only fear of pregnancy that concerned the ancient world and determined the biblical teachings. There were other factors which remain just as relevant today. One was the concern for stability of society. Marriage and the family was seen as an important context for bringing up children and for protecting women against sexual exploitation. Then there was the feeling that sexuality was a sacred area where taboos were especially appropriate. Sex connected them with very deep parts of their own being and the being of the universe.

Some of these attitudes may still have come from fear of unwanted pregnancy, but that was not the whole story. If it were, we could suggest that, in the age of safe contraception, all we really need is for people to make contracts to give stable parenting to children during their formative stages; we wouldn't need anything like marriage. But if we didn't have marriage, my hunch is that it would soon be invented. People would find some way of making public that they wanted to be a permanent couple and of asking others to recognise and respect the fact and not to interfere. The challenge of making it permanent, secure and fulfilling would be a matter for the people concerned and the ground rules would probably end up looking much like the traditional values we associate with marriage. The best marriages, to my mind, are the ones which operate something like this and are not the ones which give highest priority to claiming obligations based on formal rites. I suspect we are moving more and more away from understanding marriage as conferring rights and on to seeing it much more as a voluntary partnership of respect of equals.

Sex is powerful and connects us with life and vitality. It links us with creativity and God, not just when it leads to the creation of new human beings. It is a way of being intimate and close to another human being and out of that shared love many other things are born and created, too. Love and life reproduces love and life. The joy of sex is very close to the joy of being one with God. But what does that mean about the decisons we make about sex in an age of safe contraception?

People often say today that the most important sexual organ is the brain. In redefining our sexual practices there is one overruling guideline: care and respect for persons. Anything which depersonalises others, exploits them or treats them as things runs contrary to such loving. Whatever decisions we make, we need to make them in a context of openness and honesty and concern both for our own good and the good of others. If fear is in our thoughts we need to ask why; perhaps it is groundless and based on an irrelevant disapproval we feared once and should long since have given up; perhaps it is well-founded; we can learn from our intuitive fears. The best decisions are often those made in consultation with others who can help us keep our feet on the ground.

I have very great respect for what many in the present generation have to grapple with in the area of sexuality. In many ways I believe we could be moving to a much healthier attitude to this area of our lives. I respect that some will want to remain on the conservative side of decision making. I have the same respect for others who in care and openness explore new boundaries. Sex belongs within the context of human intimacy and caring. It is part of enjoying the way God made us. Like any other gift we can use it for good or ill, for wholeness or destruction in others and ourselves. Jesus' own teaching shifts our focus from concern with acts to concern with attitudes which is more radical.

We now have another major aspect to our caring in the area of sexuality. The arrival of AIDS has curbed the sexual euphoria of the seventies and early eighties. People have rightly become more cautious again. A healthy fear has its place here, but so does care and compassion. Both in our own personal interests and in the interests of the community as a whole we need to prevent the spread of AIDS and to show compassion to those who have contracted it, however that may have happened.

Sexual exploitation

The last two decades have also brought a greater awareness of sexual exploitation, especially of women by men, both outside of and within marriage, not to speak of child abuse and incest. We are still emerging from age old prejudices which have subordinated and often subjugated women to the whims of men. Male aggression in sexuality, whether overt or covert, is still rarely questioned in our society and lies at the base of many forms of sexual abuse. Exploitation belongs also to a much wider system which is reflected in many women holding down two jobs, one in the community and one at home, and in much more subtle attitudes, enshrined in our very language, which discounts women and women's contributions.

Christianity's adaptation, already by the later New Testament writings, of the prevailing patterns of household management in declaring the man the head of the house has contributed strongly to such attitudes. Such attitudes are deeply ingrained. They colour our language about God, our styles of decison making, our structures for decision making in the Church and the community. It has been liberating in recent years to recover Christianity's earlier radical traditions which set women and men equally side by side. The benefits of such developments are as much for men as they are for women, both generally and at the level of their sexuality.

Homosexuality and homosexual practice

One of the more turbulent areas in modern thought about sexuality is homosexuality and homosexual practice. The biblical writings reflect strong abhorrence of homosexual practice. In the world of Jesus' day homosexual love between men and young boys was a common feature of non-Jewish society; but the other forms of inter-male sexual activity were also well known and roundly condemned. One of the terms for anal intercourse, sodomy, derives from the biblical story of Sodom and Gomorrah. Apart from the fact that the traditional laws of Israel had condemned it from early days, other reasons for its rejection were its

66

unnatural pairing of two of the same sex and its exploitation of minors.

Has anything changed? Few would dispute that the argument against exploitation still stands. Some would dispute that homosexual practice is unnatural. Generally our society is much less accepting of homosexuals and homosexual practice than was the ancient non-Jewish world at the time of Jesus. My own thinking in this field has taught me to be cautious.

What if there really are people whose natural sexual preference is different from their outward physical reality? The ancient world of the biblical writers generally ignored such a possibility. What happens if we don't ignore it? Who am I to say they should try to live contrary to their natures or that they should see themselves as unfortunate accidents of nature and withhold themselves from acting out their sexual preferences with others? The issue is what is most caring for such people, not adherence to rules. How can I condemn when I - and many others who venture an opinion (including ancient biblical writers) - know so little?

If I found myself having such natural preferences, I would probably try to get them reversed to save all the hassles of living like that in today's society in the face of so much prejudice. If I found myself at some stage in my life developing stronger preferences in that direction, I would probably feel more confident about succeeding in such a reversal - I might just have suppressed my heterosexual energies for some reason. But who knows? For me, love means making room for people to make their own responsible decisions, not condemning them or haranguing them. I know some who have done just what I said I would do and have gone through hell in the process. They are committed followers of Christ, loving and caring people, and are now practising homosexuals.

Masturbation, prostitution

On other areas of sexuality like masturbation and prostitution I apply the same guidelines. The guilt that has been engendered because of the former has, to my mind, been largely a sad reflection of an unhealthy attitude towards sexuality which has affected large parts of Christianity over the centuries. Orgasm in itself is a natural and healthy life experience. I am not persuaded that self engendered orgasm harms either the person or anyone else. Older arguments about wasted seed belong to the wider view that ejaculation must always be tied to the effort to reproduce, a view which lies behind some opposition even to contraception. I would, on the contrary, see sex as being a gift God has given us to enjoy with one another. But affirming my own sexuality also means being in touch with where it is going, where it is suppressed, where it needs direction and control, where and how it needs expression.

Prostitution is another matter, largely because it seems to belong to a system of exploitation of women (sometimes, men) of which I don't want to be a part, even though prostitutes will often deny exploitation. It is not a system I want to support or encourage. Yet I also have no interest in declaring them bad people. There are many stories of very caring prostitutes - some made it into the lists of the Bible's heroes like Rahab.

Individual moral choices and laws to protect people

There is also the related question of what stand to take in the issue of legalisation of prostitution. Let me take this point as an opportunity to comment on the major difference between what people might do, themselves, and what they consider should be legally forbidden. It is important not to confuse the two. I can see that there is a case in our society for allowing legalised prostitution on the grounds that it may be a more caring way to look after all concerned than to have a system where it is practised illegally in secret locations without proper supervision and medical care and where the police cope with it by turning a blind eye. Which is the greater evil? Or, better, which way are we going to care more effectively for the people concerned? The answers to such questions are often not simple. Sometimes we have to live with the fact that we are not sure which is the appropriate action. In such borderline decisions we need a maximum of knowledge, tolerance and care. Dogmatic authoritarian assertions are least helpful when dealing with matters of such sensitivity.

Another complex issue is abortion. Here differing concerns compete. What is more important: the life of the foetus or the life of the mother? When does the child's life begin in the womb or when should it be considered a human being? What constitutes danger to the life of the mother: death? psychological trauma? social deprivation? I respect those who hold to absolutes here: life must not be taken under any circumstances. Yet I am unhappy with it as a fixed rule. I have the deepest respect for people who grapple with the issue at a practical level. I want to support people making decisions in full integrity, seeking the most caring way forward and I think that, given the complexities of many cases, I would not help the situation with foregone conclusions. I would certainly want our legislation to leave some flexibility for personal decision, but that also means setting some limit beyond which society must say no.

Setting boundaries and preserving individual freedom

At many points society must say no and restrict the freedom of individuals in the interests of the whole. We need such rules as well as guidelines. They are there to protect people's interests, to set outer limits against actions which cause harm to society as a whole or to people not otherwise able to protect themselves. These are the outer boundaries. We need them. We need speed limits on our roads, acceptable blood alcohol levels, laws to regulate commercial life and so on. We need a system which enforces these society limits and a system for dealing with those who transgress them, a system which deters by punishment and which seeks reform and protects society from wilful harm.

Setting these outer boundaries goes a long way towards shaping the way we live together as a community. Caring about people means caring about these. This means having a lively interest in what is going on in the wider community. Are the limits being set in ways that allow some to exploit others? Is everyone being given a fair go? In his day Jesus focused especially on those who had little voice or power in community decision making and called his followers to be a voice for them and with them. This is why the Church, where it has its act together, is out front on issues of justice, poverty, protection of minority groups, respect for human rights.

In setting the outer boundaries of society we are defining right and wrong only in the broadest sense. True, if you cheat the rest of the community by holding back your contribution to the common purse (your tax), you can be caught and punished, but mostly the boundaries are set so wide that some levels of cheating, lying, deceit, exploitation, are all possible with little check on them. You can't legislate against selfishness and greed. You can't legislate to make people loving. You also shouldn't try to. People need freedom to make their decisions.

Trying to force people to be a sharing and caring society was the ideal of communism and it failed. People do things best if they do them because they want to. That is why the western capitalist society, based on letting people pursue their own interests, works better: they have more room to do what they want to do and so to do things with energy and enthusiasm and therefore with efficiency. But that means, of course, leaving room for people to be simply selfish and greedy. That is the

69

negative risk of granting so much freedom. This means that society must also act responsibly to counter exploitation by the selfish and greedy and to support the disadvantaged and the poor. Left to its own devices the free market economy will inevitably widen the gap between the rich and the poor. Therefore enlightened and caring governments will establish structures which combine control, on the one hand, with room for initiative and reward, on the other.

With such limits I want to protect people's right to such room, but that makes it all the more urgent that I am aware that it is quite another question how I as a Christian use that free space. To follow Jesus means to use the space between the boundaries to live for love and that is quite opposite to how our western system of economics assumes people will use it and to why the system works.

Complex ethical issues

Back at the boundaries, today we are facing many very difficult new decisions on right and wrong. How free, for instance, should scientists be to experiment with human embryos? When should medical treatment cease in the case of terminally ill patients? Should such patients have the right to terminate their own lives? What about animal experimentation? How far should the community sacrifice its forests and natural flora and fauna for the sake of exploiting new resources for the community's needs? Can we afford to allow our cities to grow as they have? What limits should we impose on industries to curtail polluting gases in the environment? What role should our community have in arms manufacture? Is nuclear energy a responsible energy alternative? Should uranium be exported when there is only a limited assurance that it will not one day be used in nuclear weapons? Should pure heroin be made available to users to counteract the dangers which arise from use of impure heroin and the criminality and exploitation rampant in the illicit drug trade? How far should the community restrict sale and advertising of cigarettes? Should marajuana be legalised?

I cannot discuss these questions here, but they belong to the wide range of issues of right and wrong with which we must grapple. In approaching them our guidelines are few. They all flow from concern for people and include some of the following questions: Are the solutions in the long term interest of the world and its people? Is an adequate data base being considered? Have the possible effects on people and their environment been considered? Are the voices of those directly affected being heard clearly? Are the questions being asked in a way which ignores or excludes other relevant issues?

The Church, at its best, addresses some of these issues and sometimes risks, for the sake of love, its own solutions, which may or may not prove appropriate. Safe silence in so many of these would be a betrayal of care. Often people, including many Church people, resent the Church's having its say. In reality in most cases it is an elected body or a representative who issues a statement. It ought to be seen as only that and not more than that, as though the person or elected body were claiming to be able to express the view of every member, let alone, with absolute certainty the view of God! Yet the often fierce resistance which we encounter seems to hark back to just such an understanding of the Church (that it speaks for God and so claims infallibility). In most of these issues the Church as such has no particular expertise and joins the conversation primarily because of its concern for people and the world. It deserves to be heard, I believe, because of the long tradition of wisdom and love it represents.

Many of the issues noted above belong to the so-called 'grey areas' facing our community, where dogmatic assertions simply do not help. These issues need full discussion with adequate information and the willingness to take risks. Strong controversy aids the process if it means all angles and details are carefully explored. At its best our parliamentary system of Government and Opposition parties serves the process of exploration well. The preferable process of decision making is one where every person is heard and respected and where people share a concern to work together for the good of all.

Fear of facing complex issues

Some people find such processes difficult and want someone to tell them simply what is right and what is wrong. In the wider community they want a heavy handed government or a 'right thinking' dictator. In a Christian context they claim the Bible has all the answers or that the person who prays will know God's will. I believe this is simply not true. Occasionally we may be fairly confident of God's will for us, although even then it is wise to check our perceptions with others; but often we do not know, and to pretend to know on the basis of misguided piety is delusory and can be very dangerous. Religions which have set answers of rights and wrongs have plenty of customers. But they are often, to my mind, an escape from reality. At the very personal level of individual living we often face 'grey areas' on decisions such as which job we should apply for, where we should live and with whom. We need to trust ourselves to make decisions and be caring and tolerant of our mistakes. We don't need to walk around full of fears and surrounded by guilt.

Disappearing 'don'ts'

I can only welcome the disappearance of so many of the 'don't's that characterised Christianity and smile at them now: don't gamble, don't drink, don't dance, don't go to the movies, don't smoke, don't play sport on Sundays. It now seems all so trivial, especially since I could take all that so seriously and yet have no idea what the bigger issues of life, like justice and peace and poverty, were about. It was just like the people of whom Jesus said that they strained out a small fly only to swallow a camel. I don't mean to imply that none of those 'don't' areas is relevant. There are quite a few where dangers to health and wholeness still lurk, not least in smoking, but hardly in dancing, movies and sport on Sundays!

There are bigger issues of right and wrong which have less to do with keeping petty rules and regulations and more to do with compassion for fellow human beings and care for the environment. It is the compassion I see lived out in the life of Jesus that is my starting point for thinking about right and wrong. Inspired by Jesus' approach, I like to think of God sometimes as being like a wise old woman or man, full of understanding and also of no-nonsense caring. Such a one looks upon our struggles in decision making with eager compassion, understands our mistakes, stays with us in new ventures, has all the patience in the world as we learn to love and the sadness and anger when we don't and shut ourselves off; but is always there, ready to listen, to comfort and to challenge.

There are, however, many situations in life, where we do not have time to think over our decisions and weigh our alternatives. And many of the things we do are determined not by what we think but by what we feel and what we are. So the kind of person we are is an important component in our thinking about right and wrong. In the same way in our society many wrong actions must be seen as part of a longer process which reflects something being wrong in society itself. When we see kids sniffing petrol and adults abusing themselves with alcohol, we need also to ask what has been going wrong in society that people make self destructive choices like these. When we do, we will often find a whole history of violence and abuse which has robbed communities and people of their self respect. Ask any Aboriginal Australian!

Ultimately discussion of right and wrong, whether in relation to individuals or to communities, needs to consider much more than what people do. It needs to consider how things are. This is why being Christian is more than being concerned with doing right or wrong. It is about a way of being, both as individuals and as a community, as I hope to show in the final chapter.

ooo
___

The Sadducees' Question

a sequel (Luke 20:27-38)

'In the resurrection, therefore, whose wife will the woman be?' (20:33)

The story waits to be told. The angel Gabriel sensed what was at stake. The brothers were there, befuddled with their competing claims to the one woman. Who would possess her in the resurrection? Gabriel suspended the metamorphosis, presenting before them instead only a doll like semblance of the woman. They each rushed towards her, claiming their rights. A struggle developed among them. One tore an arm; another a leg, oblivious of the kapok filling which spilled at their feet.

Blind in their possessive greed, they each ripped for themselves their claim. One went off taking an arm carefully secured, placed it in a drawer. Another pinned his portion up by the calendars. Between them they had everything and they had nothing.

The next day the seven brothers appeared at the market. There suddenly before them stood Judith herself. This time it was different. As one stepped forward, hands were stretched out, fingers touched, and in a moment both were transformed into doves, busy, beside each other, together finding scraps under the market tables, flying upward when disturbed. As the second stepped forward, hands stretched out and fingers touched, they were transformed into two dolphins, beside each other in the shining water, leaping up, diving down again, swirling in the deep. Soon there also two sheep, two parrots, two lizards, two dogs, two magpies.

The crowds who had been watching saw everything and saw nothing. People had gathered to celebrate the coming together, but soon all seven brothers were gone and Judith who had once appeared had also vanished. Some muttered about the system and the one who wouldn't even let a disciple attend his father's funeral, disrupted families leaving old men to run fishing businesses and to tidy the books of their tax collecting sons.

Then an old woman stepped forward, resting on her old walking stick and peering out over the gathered crowd. She still had voice and addressed them. 'Abraham,' she said, 'Isaac, and you, Jacob, and the rest of you, why do you stand around here so curious? There is no place in this kingdom for possession. I belong neither to first nor to last. I never did; that was your imagining. There is a holiness undefined by boundaries, a faithfulness unmeasured by performance, an intimacy untouched by the strongest bonds of commitment. It is a leaving of family and a finding of family, a leaving of father and mother and a finding of father and mother, a being born to a higher and deeper reality of love which goes far beyond the worlds of duty, claim and rights and more than fulfills them.'

The celebrations began, an ancient dance, a circle. As each round was performed, one would lead and another follow until each had led and each had danced, some with flourish, some hobbling, some with screams of delight, some engrossed in an eternal rhythm of mystery. The brothers were there in the dance, each taking his turn. There was room for everyone.

The festivities went on into the night. Near midnight one frail young man entered the market place, sack on shoulder. The crowd gathered around him. He made a table upright, emptied the dried fish onto it and the loaves, poured the wine and with pierced hands invited them to share.

Yes, they all came, some very hesitant, some confused, even a little angry at not having understood. Even the doves flew down for the crumbs. The parrots and magpies screeched and squawked like it was already morning. The dogs barked. The sheep ate what was left of the kapok on the ground. Lizards scurried beneath upturned tables and down near the beach the dolphins simply continued to rise and fall in the magic of the waters. It was soon morning. The light had come. Jesus packed up his bag and went off for another day.

ooo

What about being Christian ?

Dear Kim

There seem to be so many ideas around about what it means to be Christian. Some people think its means being 'good'; others speak about being 'born again'; others, about belonging to a Christian country; and others, about being 'christened'.

Being 'christened'?

Christenings or baptisms might be a good place to start. It used to be the case that nearly everyone was baptised; it was one of the things 'proper' parents did for their kids. It still is in some countries. But in Australia and New Zealand it's become less common. What difference does a Church ceremony which sprinkles water on the heads of small babies make, anyway, we might ask.

For some people it made a huge difference and still does: it's the difference between being pagan and Christian, between going to hell or going to heaven. For them, baptism is a kind of magic which makes you one thing or the other. It is hard to imagine, but for some people it made all the difference. There is often a strange idea of God behind all this. God will get upset if the person has not been 'done' - enough to want to punish them for eternity. I see this as a very sincere but also very sick idea of God. God is not finnicky. What sort of decent parent or human being would want to stand on ceremony in this way? Once again, out-moded ideas of what used to count as appropriate for 'superior' human beings have been foisted onto our idea of God and have stuck.

Being sprinkled with water or being dipped in water cannot make that kind of difference. But I like the image of water in thinking about God. God is like the water that brings life to dry places, the water which quenches our thirst, the water that washes; and being in touch with God is like standing in a stream of life which has flowed down through history. The life of Jesus is like the main head waters, though other springs flow into the stream as well.

I like to think of baptism as an act which represents my joining that stream or putting myself (or my children) in the place where it flows. The stream flows where you find people gathered together enjoying its waters. That will be in local congregations and groups where people come together to open themselves to the kind of life Jesus showed. When parents want their children to be in the place where the stream flows, then baptising children makes a lot of sense. I couldn't want anything less for children than that they be surrounded with the kind of influence which comes down from Jesus. However going through the act of baptism where this is not intended makes a mockery of it. Unfortunately baptism as 'the social thing to do' often lost sight of its deeper meaning.

Being sprinkled with water or being immersed in water, which is more dramatic and the more ancient form of baptism, is nothing on its own; but, when we associate it with these deeper meanings, it can be a wonderful symbol. That will often entail bringing that meaning back to an event we, ourselves, cannot remember and which may have happened without much thought. That is like a lot of life's experiences - including, of course, our own birth!

The earliest Christians always linked coming to believe in the gospel with this symbolic act, so much so that often it could stand for the whole process of conversion. For instance, instead of saying something like, 'When we opened ourselves to Christ and his influence, we became part of him and his influence and we symbolised that by being baptised', Paul could simply say: we were 'baptised into Christ.' That was shorthand.

Shorthand expressions

Shorthand expressions like this can be quite useful, but also quite confusing. One of the most famous sayings attributed to Jesus is one about being 'born again': 'Unless people are born again, they cannot see the kingdom of God'; or 'Unless people are born of water and the Spirit, they cannot enter the kingdom of God.' Inevitably some people began to use shorthand like: by water or baptism we become children of God. If you forget that this is shorthand, it sounds like people become children of God simply by going through a water ceremony, as if it had some magical quality of its own.

Properly understood, it means that when you become 'Christian', you join yourself to Jesus and his movement. This is a new beginning. It means opening yourself to what he was on about and joining others who are on about the same thing. You can seal this by going through baptism or, for people who have been baptised once before, by reaffirming what your baptism symbolised.

'Born again'

But it is not just around baptism that there has been a lot of confusion. I've already mentioned the term 'born again'. It's become a hackneyed phrase and can mean almost anything: 'he's a born again marketer'; 'she's a born again saleswoman'. In these expressions it seems to mean: being full of enthusiasm. Unfortunately, it has been Christians of a strongly fundamentalist kind (who treat the Bible almost like a magical book) who have used 'born again' a lot. For many people, 'born again' Christians are those who are especially fanatical and rigid. For this reason, I am rather reluctant to use the term any more. People get the wrong idea.

The original idea is linked with changing life direction, turning around and beginning again. It's more, though, than turning over a new leaf, because it means also something has happened, has been done to me, to make me able to change. When I let go worrying about what people think of me or feeling guilty and inadequate and believe what Jesus said, that God loves me, then that can really turn me around. We can be transformed inside and out.

There are famous stories of people, like Paul, who changed from being someone wanting to stamp out the early Christian movement to one of its strongest proponents - quite sensational and dramatic. But for other people the influence of Jesus is just something that grows on them until they find they are more Christian than anything else. It doesn't matter how; the important thing is choosing to open ourselves to the kind of God Jesus talked about and showed us.

It is not the label 'Christian' that matters; it was a nickname given to Christians because they talked about Christ. What matters is not what we are called but what we are and what we want to be. Becoming Christian is only the beginning of a process of letting ourselves be more and more shaped by love and concern for others and by a close relationship with God.

Going to heaven or going to hell?

Often people think the main thing about becoming Christian is making sure you get to heaven when you die. If you're a Christian, if you've made a decision to follow Christ, then you'll be saved; if you haven't, you won't. But this kind of thinking skews what Christianity is about. It puts a far off place in the centre of things and encourages me to think only of myself. It also puts far too much weight on the single event of making a decision. How can a decision once made or an experience of conversion function as a kind of guarantee like that? Doesn't life here and now matter? As I read Jesus, relationships matter most - both in the here and now and in the future. Being a Christian is about living in touch with God. It is about my relationship with God and so with people, with myself, and with the world around me. God is at the centre of it all, not heaven or hell.

What about heaven and hell then? How should we think about them? I find the idea of hell as a place where God punishes people forever and ever a repugnant idea. It contradicts the image of God as loving and caring which I find at the centre of Jesus' teaching. The idea of God's loving as a kind of temporary concession in history would give me finally a God who ceases to care. We would not tolerate any system of justice which proposed permanent torture. Even our most severe sentences leave room for reform and rehabilitation. This 'god' leaves no room.

Yet, for all that, the image of hell can be useful as an image of human chaos and destruction. People can create their own hell, even hell on earth, and can do so for others. In creation God makes room for our reality and that includes making room for us to destroy ourselves and to make hell for ourselves and others. Cutting ourselves off from God's love and wisdom, becoming alienated from God's being, estranged from our inner home, is also a hell we can make for ourselves.

Some Christians pretend their way around the Bible in order to agree with the kind of position I am arguing. They refuse to acknowledge the rough parts. I think it is more honest to acknowledge that there are biblical passages which espouse the kind of belief in hell which I am rejecting. I have no difficulty in this because I am not suggesting we treat the Bible as infallible.

What about heaven? Heaven and hell belong to a complex cluster of images which people used when they tried to think about life with God beyond this life. The earliest Christians, like the Jews of the time, had a wide range of ideas about such life. One common image was of heaven as the invisible realm where God sat on a throne and ruled the universe assisted by angels. The spirits or souls of good people were also in heaven, either asleep or fully aware of events above and below. Frequently God's presence was pictured as dazzling, bright light. People spoke of heaven as a place of great beauty and wonderful music. These are all images, such as we might find in our dreams. They are ways of saying that God is God and to be close to God is the most wonderful thing imaginable. Heaven is the language of poetry - so is hell.

Life after death?

But what about life after death? Some people try to prove this by recounting so-called contacts with the dead through spiritualism or by noting what people report who have technically died for some minutes and then been revived and who speak of out of the body experiences. It seems that it is common for such people to report strong sensations of well-being, of meeting significant people of their past and of seeing bright lights. Perhaps this is a form of hallucination. Possibly there is more to it. Then there are phenomena such as extra sensory perception or long distance mental communication which seem to suggest other levels of reality, but at most these make me doubt the sufficiency of current scientific hypotheses.

Yet in the choice between denying or affirming life after death, I come down on the side of belief. My starting point is God and I am confident that in death I am not cut off from God. I believe that, as with Jesus, I go to be with God. I don't think I need to know any more. God is enough; the rest is imagery. In making this affirmation I am going far beyond what can be proved and you may feel I am believing too much. I ought to be able to say more than I can about how I envisage the relationship between the human body and brain and such life without body and brain. I certainly envisage a continuity of awareness (I will know this is me!). I do not mean simply a carry over of life force or impersonal soul into some other being such as in the ideas of reincarnation which hold so much fascination for many, because I don't really understand that as living. I will not know this is me.

A vision to live by

But there is another set of images about the future which are much more powerful for me. These belong within the framework of thought about a future kingdom of God and about a second coming of Jesus. Do I believe in the second coming? I can't answer that with a simple yes or no. I need first to say what I understand these terms to mean.

Jesus spoke of the kingdom of God or God's reign as something people could look forward to. He said the poor and hungry could be glad because of the hope it would bring. They would be fed. They would find

80

justice and peace. The current power structures in the world would be changed. There would be room for the outcast and despised. The powers that oppress people within themselves and within the wider human community would be removed. Jesus picked up the imagery of the prophets who spoke of men and women from all the peoples of the earth coming together in peace, beating their swords into plows and their spears into pruning hooks. One common image he used for this was of a meal in which all would share.

Jesus taught his disciples to pray: Your kingdom come! Yet he did more than this. He took his image of hope as an agenda for living here and now. In his life he showed God's generosity; he included outcasts; he affirmed the worth of people of different race; he showed God's acceptance and love towards the least loveable in society. And one of the characteristic ways in which this happened was by his taking the unusual step of eating meals with them. That meant departing from the normal custom of not eating with those considered unworthy or unacceptable in society. By using meals to show his openness and acceptance towards outcasts, Jesus made them into a kind of advance statement of how the world was to be. They showed Jesus living out future hope in the present.

As we saw in the chapter on Jesus, Jesus' last meal was seen as the culmination of such meals and the starting point of the Christian practice of Holy Communion. The earliest believers met regularly for such meals. In them, on the one hand, they remembered Jesus (it became a memorial meal) and, on the other hand, they celebrated in advance the day when the kingdom of God would come fully and they would be joined again by Jesus. Very quickly they spoke of sensing Jesus' being present with them when they ate the meal together. The Lord's Supper, as it came to be called, became a holy 'communion' or fellowship with him as well as an act of thanksgiving (the meaning of the word 'Eucharist') for his life. And in celebrating it they also looked forward to Jesus' return.

Thus in the hands of his first disciples Jesus' hope and vision for the future came to include also a hope about him. Here is where the so called second coming of Jesus fits in. They hoped for the kingdom's coming and continued to pray in the Lord's prayer: your kingdom come! They also hoped to see Jesus again and prayed: Marana tha! (Aramaic for: Our Lord come!). The first generations of Christians even believed that this hope would reach its fulfilment within a short time. Paul seems to have thought it would be in his lifetime! Jesus probably left it very open, but must have left behind the impression that fulfilment was not far away.

Urgent hope

This had a lot to do with the political and social crises which the Jews were living through at the time. Roman suppression of their religious movements and exploitation of their land through heavy taxes meant that many were reaching the breaking point of desperation. Surely history could not go on like this! Christianity was born in this atmosphere and its hopes were not easily separable from the cry for religious and political liberation. Certainly Jesus' hope seems to have envisaged the kind of practical transformation of society which would be good news for the poor, for his fellow Jews in Galilee.

Unlike Jesus, some of his fellow Jews opted for armed rebellion. They succeeded in instigating a major revolt against Rome in 66-70 AD. The result was a disaster. The temple was destroyed. That kind of Judaism was all but finished and certainly met its end half a century later when the city was levelled. It was left for the surviving Jews who did not join the great revolt to reconstitute Judaism and lay the foundations for the Judaism we know today.

New twists in the urge for change

Meanwhile Christianity was finding it had a much greater following among non-Jews than among Jews. Visions and images of hope were becoming progressively disentangled from their Jewish nationalist roots. This development had the potential to unleash a movement living for justice and peace in every society. It also had the potential to transform Christianity into a movement no longer concerned with such an earthly fulfilment of the kingdom of God, but focused primarily on the individual and on the spiritual world. In history both options have at times been taken. On the one hand, we see Christians, already in the first century, transferring God's reign into the invisible world of heaven or the soul. Hope becomes escape from this world into the next by death or during this life by mystical contemplation. But, on the other, at its best, we can also see Christianity offering a universally valid lifestyle, combining a deep sense of oneness with God in prayer and community with a practical devotion to live out the vision of the kingdom in everyday life.

Feeding on life and hope - in the community

Looking back on all of this, I find the simple eating of bread and drinking of wine at Holy Communion an event which tells me without words who I am and what I am about. It connects me with the vision of Jesus and with my life agenda. It feeds me with what he was and is. Eating and drinking becomes a symbolic way of opening myself again to that simple, yet profound love that matters most. It also connects me with all others who feed on this food and seek to live in this way.

I do this with others in community, usually in a church. I don't pretend that the others with me are saints or that they understand things the way I do. And sometimes things can go on which make me feel quite of place. But that is what it means to drink at this stream. I am not a saint either. I am not always appropriate. I don't mean I just have to sit back and put up with things I might not find helpful in the church; I can say something; so can others. But I am celebrating something which says there is a place here for every one of us.

Yet I also have understanding when people sometimes say it is asking too much to stay with a congregation where we need to make an enormous effort each time to connect with the heart of the gospel. On the one hand, I can get worried about people shopping around for a comfortable church congregation. Looking for people who are just like me or who fit in with my ideas may entail surrendering an important aspect of the gospel: that there is room for all here. But, on the other hand, when one gets the message that something other than the gospel is predominating - such as fundamentalism, narrow mindedness, mutual comfort of the comfortable without commitment to justice, ideology and activism without spirituality - then why continue to offer support?

Belonging to Christ in the Church

A number of the people to whom I feel closest are either just in or just out of the Church - at least that is how many see them. Those 'many' would perhaps see themselves as church stalwarts, whereas I might see them as having lost contact with what I see as central. I think it is a major tragedy that more and more people who are genuinely on the side of Jesus in what matters most find no room in the Church. They have been encouraged to think that the norm in the Church is a naive pietism which treats the Bible as infallible, has narrow moral views and largely right wing political tendencies and discourages intellectual integrity. I want to say to them, that the Church is where the stream flows; don't leave the heritage of Jesus to the fundamentalists and narrow religious people. That is to abandon him to his opponents.

And I would want to say to those who with great dedication help maintain the institutional structures of the Church: beware of compromising the faith for the sake of apparent unity! Lowest common denominator Christianity will inevitably pander to conservative religionists. Hold the boundaries wide open for diversity with integrity! I know in myself the tension between the will to compromise and not offend and the challenge of faith integrity. In ecumenical relations we push our creativity to the limits. I sometimes wonder whether in putting some things into acceptable formulations I have not blurred significant edges. The Church needs to be a place where there is room for diversity and struggle in the search for truth. My picture of God in all this is not of a nail biting deity, but of one who is glad human beings are using their minds.

Other religions?

So far I have not said anything about other religions or about more recent movements which seek to explore the spiritual meaning of life. I return to my imagery of the rug from chapter 2. The light shines through the rug at many points in human history. I have no interest in defining boundaries on the rug. If light shines in and through another religion or movement, and I have no doubt that it does, then I can only be glad. I will join hands with all who live by that light.

But, having said that, what do I mean by light? I mean by light the light that is God and my starting point in understanding that light is Jesus. It is the light as I see it in Jesus that I am welcoming. I don't mean light with a Christian label; light doesn't wear labels. I mean the light that shows itself in unconditional, affirming love for people and care and respect for the world around us. That is the love I have met in Jesus. I will not shy away from meeting it anywhere else and will rejoice wherever I find it.

I know from my limited reading that that light shines through at many points in the great religious and philosophical traditions of humankind and in many modern movements of spirituality. I know also that there are many points where I would see that light dimmed or darkened, including within Christian traditions. Whatever dehumanises, whatever causes people to be treated as of lesser worth than others, whatever disparages or is destructive of the created world, blocks that light. And whoever lives by the light which affirms what I see God affirming in Jesus is my spiritual companion. And when I don't know where my fellow human being in another religion is going, I will want to listen and not judge.

The world needs you

The world needs men and women who can live with sensitivity to God in their lives. We don't need any more people claiming to have all the answers or claiming to be better than everyone else. We need people who will decide to live at one with God, the loving God we learn of in Jesus. This is more than an internal private commitment; it is a decision to live with others and to be in community. It is to join up with others walking the same road. It means standing in the stream, being within the life of the Church, sharing its great resources, struggling sometimes where its channels are blocked and living out its hope in the world.

Christian living also includes developing private habits which stimulate our sensitivity to God's love in ourselves and our world and being quite deliberate about it. Here, there are no rules. We must find what works for us. People find a number of things helpful: guided Bible reading; reading to keep informed of current issues; reading poetry, drama, novels; finding insights through film and theatre; enjoying and expressing oneself through various forms of art or music; enjoying nature and beauty; meeting with other human beings who challenge us or simply bring us love and joy; meditating, perhaps using relaxation strategies of thought and body movement; praying, using written prepared ordered material or in spontaneous self expression - thinking out loud before God, writing down personal reflections and challenges.

Ultimately being Christian has little to do with labels or status. It is not about guarantees or special spiritual favours. It is not even particularly religious. It is sometimes most real where the term, 'Christian', isn't even mentioned. It is about a way of being human, of being what we were made to be. And that means living at one with God, in love and compassion towards other human beings and ourselves, and with care for the universe in which we live.

Conclusion

Dear Kim

I have written all this because I want you to know what I really believe. I have tried to be as clear and direct as possible and to set aside thoughts of what people might expect me to say or believe. I know you will sense my enthusiasm; some areas about which I have written are closely connected to what I teach in my work. But some are simply my reflections about faith at this stage of my life journey. I think I can say that most of what I have written here has been my belief for at least the last twenty-five years. Yet there are some areas where my views and attitudes have changed and doubtless will change. I am sharing what I believe in the hope that you and others may find it a stimulus for your own reflections.

There is more than enthusiasm behind what I have written. There are people. I have learned so much through my relationships with my fellow human beings. People are full of mystery. Human beings are extraordinary. Beyond all the words, the appearances, the movements, and yet connected with them, is a thinking, feeling, reflecting being in each person. I can approach, meet, encounter another human being, yet, beyond all I can meet, there is so much more which I don't know. There is a sacredness, a holy space of inner being which I can sense only at a distance.

It is as though each person is a sacred temple and we meet mostly only in the outer courts. There are special moments when being with someone is more than this. And then there are also moments when, by entering within my own deep inner sense of sacredness, I find myself at one, not only with myself, but also with others and with God. That has little to do with how I feel and a lot to do with what I believe or, better, with what I allow to be.

This deep mystery I share with all other human beings, for I believe that this sacred space is within each of us. When I picture this sacred space as a holy temple, I am aware of entering it in company. There I am never alone. There I find many people. Jesus is there; so are men and women from history. It is Jesus who helps me make sense of what the

86

space is all about. When I listen for God, it is his voice I hear, sometimes in clear tones, sometimes muffled through the cries of human beings in need.

The temple is decorated with panels of faith, the rich traditions of the Bible, the stories of love and courage. The sacred space is filled with all kinds of people, some like me, some very unlike me, some with whom I feel awkward, some comfortable to be with. Yet there is room for them all. The space is not crowded.

Like a dream, the picture is not constant. Sometimes the holy space is not within a temple at all; it is in someone's living room or on a street or in a prison. Sometimes I am right there in what is happening; other times I am observing from far away. The holiness has nothing to do with being stuck up and proud. It is there when Jesus touches the leper, sits down with Mary, takes a meal with the rogue, Zacchaeus, lifts the children to his lap, confronts the chief priests. The holy space is there even without people: in the hills, the forests, the oceans. It is there when they are replenished and cared for and when they cry out for preservation.

Sometimes the sacred space is filled with silence, wonder at all that is, a kind of still enjoyment of God's presence. At other times there are voices of concern, conflicting voices, uncertain sounds as people confront new decisions. Some decisions are made in the dark, resolutions worked through on scant evidence, ventures undertaken without the advantage of precedent. The sacred space has room for abandoned experiments, discarded models, broken constructs.

Being in touch with all of this is being in touch with love. It is love which is the sacred energy, the sacred space, the place which makes room for life to go on and which ultimately made room for life to come into being in the beginning. Love was there in the beginning and will be there in the end. It is this love, which is the life of God and which shone through Jesus, which is also there for us in the present.

There is nothing greater that I can wish for, for myself or for you or for anyone else, than to discover that love and be discovered by it. Finding this is finding ourselves and finding one another and, ultimately, it is finding God. This is not a single moment in time, but a sacred space in which to live. It is the sacred space of love and compassion, there for all to enter and for all to share. It is the invitation of God. This is what I believe.

87